Praise for *Five-Minute Relationship Repair*

"This wise and practical book brilliantly addresses the core issues that need attention in order for couples and individuals to create deeply fulfilling relationships. Through vivid examples, incisive commentary, and helpful exercises, the authors take us on a journey that leads toward a richer understanding of ourselves and others. Incorporating attachment theory and the latest discoveries in neuroscience, this book offers an astonishingly clear path toward the love and intimacy we long for."

— **John Amodeo, PhD**, author of *Dancing with Fire*

"This book, written for both singles and couples, shows us how to approach differences with openhearted listening and vulnerable truth-telling. It presents a step-by-step process for using any relationship conflict as a doorway to deeper intimacy and expanded awareness. It is readable and entertaining as well as extremely practical. Readers are given worksheets that teach them exactly what to say and do when someone gets emotionally triggered or reactive. If you read and work with the practices offered here, you have everything you need to create a secure, lasting bond with your partner."

— **Jack Canfield**, coauthor of *The Success Principles*™
and *Chicken Soup for the Couple's Soul*

"*Five-Minute Relationship Repair* should be of help to anyone wishing to repair an ailing relationship. Using the case of a typical couple in trouble as their starting point, John Grey and Susan Campbell walk you through a sequential set of techniques based on neuroscience and attachment theory. With decades of experience behind them, Grey and Campbell are highly intelligent, creative forces in the field of science and relationships. Their work here is inventive, inspiring, and well worth the read.

— **Stan Tatkin, PsyD, MFT**, author of *Wired for Love,*
Your Brain on Love, and *Love and War in Intimate Relationships*

Five-Minute Relationship Repair

Five-Minute Relationship Repair

Quickly Heal Upsets, Deepen Intimacy, and Use Differences to Strengthen Love

Susan Campbell, PhD, *and* John Grey, PhD

H J Kramer

published in a joint venture with

New World Library
Novato, California

An H J Kramer book

published in a joint venture with

New World Library

Editorial office:
H J Kramer Inc.
PO Box 1082
Tiburon, California 94920

Administrative office:
New World Library
14 Pamaron Way
Novato, California 94949

Text design by Tona Pearce Myers

Library of Congress Cataloging-in-Publication Data
Campbell, Susan M., date.
Five-minute relationship repair : quickly heal upsets, deepen intimacy, and use differences to strengthen love / Susan Campbell & John Grey.
    pages   cm
"Published in a joint venture with New World Library."
Includes index.
ISBN 978-1-932073-71-3 (pbk. : alk. paper) — ISBN 978-1-932073-72-0 (ebook)
1. Man-woman relationships. 2. Interpersonal relations. 3. Interpersonal conflict. 4. Couples—Psychology. I. Grey, John, date. II. Title.
HQ801.A3C35 2015   306.7—dc23

First printing, February 2015
ISBN 978-1-932073-71-3
Printed in Canada on 100% postconsumer-waste recycled paper

10   9   8   7   6   5   4   3   2   1

Contents

Introduction

FALLING IN LOVE IS THE EASY PART. Staying in love is another matter. Some couples seem blessed with everlasting love. Then there's the rest of us — who start running into trouble once the honeymoon is over. We encounter differences, disagreements, disappointments. Buttons get pushed. We watch helplessly as loving feelings start to fade in the face of misunderstandings, blowups, shutdowns, or vicious communication cycles.

What do couples blessed with ongoing happiness know that we don't know? In a word, they know how to *repair*. They are good at quickly attending to the little glitches that every relationship encounters. Those of us who do not naturally know how to do this suffer a buildup over time of unrepaired ruptures. Eventually this buildup leads to feeling unsafe or guarded with each other. And we find ourselves feeling less intimate, less relaxed, and often more alone.

This gradual erosion of loving feelings is extremely common — so common that it could be considered normal. But what if there were another path you could take with your partner? What if you knew how to repair upsets skillfully and quickly? What if you could learn to approach relationship ruptures in a way that deepens intimacy and makes you feel more secure? The ability to repair like this is a skill you can learn. And once you learn this skill, you can do it in five minutes!

This book teaches you a step-by-step process that addresses the root causes of the frustrations and hurts that get triggered in a relationship. You will learn how to use any upset as a doorway to mutual healing and deeper trust. If you are currently in a relationship, you can immediately put these tools into practice with your partner. If you are single, you can use them to heal wounds from past relationships and prepare yourself for a successful loving partnership. Partnered or not, you can use these tools to improve communication with all the significant people in your life.

By the time you finish reading and doing the exercises offered here, you will:

❖ understand what really causes blowups, shutdowns, stuckness, and vicious cycles (it's not what you thought it was).

❖ know how to defuse conflicts and get back to feeling close.

❖ know how to help your partner calm down and listen to you even when he or she is upset.

❖ be able to ask for what you want in ways that will be well-received.

❖ be able to make sure your connection with your partner does not get compromised by hidden resentments or unfinished business.

❖ know how to help your partner feel secure with you so he or she is less likely to get triggered.

❖ know how to work with your own unfinished emotional business and past wounds in a way that promotes greater self-love and self-esteem.

❖ start rewiring your brain so that you are less apt to get triggered.

❖ have a well-practiced formula for making up after a fight or misunderstanding in a way that deepens your shared love, trust, and sense of safety.

We have named this formula the *Five-Minute Relationship Repair*. It is a step-by-step procedure you can do in five minutes or less — once you have gone through all the exercises in this book.

The early chapters show you how the nervous system is connected to emotions and why people tend to get triggered so easily by an unintentional act from an intimate partner. In these chapters, you will learn how to spot the early warning signs that someone is triggered and how to immediately pause to calm yourselves and come back to being present.

Next, a series of exercises will help you communicate about difficult or upset feelings in a way that evokes empathy from your partner. You will learn the distinction between core feelings (which are soft, tender, and vulnerable) and reactive feelings (which come across as aggressive, defensive, hard, or protective). You will see that many of the upsets you experience are based on complete misunderstandings. And you will learn why taking responsibility for your own reactions is one of the healthiest things you can do for yourself and your relationship.

The final chapters take you even deeper into learning how to heal the fears and sensitivities that give rise to frustrating communication cycles and patterns. There you will put it all together — everything you have learned about why you react and what you really need from your partner — into the Five-Minute Relationship Repair process. This section includes fill-in-the-blank scripts that guide you and your partner in getting to the root of any upset and resolving it. Saying each script to each other removes all sense of threat or blame, replacing defensiveness with open-hearted self-disclosure and loving reassurances.

Are you ready? Ready to reprogram all the unfortunate reactive habits you've picked up over the years? Ready to start anew with yourself or with a partner, living in a way that continually deepens your capacity for love and trust?

Okay. Let the healing of old patterns and learning of new tools begin — making way for a life of shared happiness and lasting love.

Exercises, Appendices, and Free Online Workbook

There are various important exercises throughout this book. Each will help you learn the tools we present and apply them to your circumstances. To make it easier for you to do these exercises, we have compiled them into one convenient, well-organized workbook. You can download and print this for free, our gift to you. We will frequently refer to the online workbook and suggest you use it in doing the exercises. Utilizing it will enhance your ability to integrate these new tools into your life.

Additionally, we have created two appendices to help you. Appendix A summarizes important scripts you will be using for repairing upsets. Appendix B offers lists of words you can use to fill in the blanks in some of the key exercises in this book. For ease of use, these appendices are duplicated in your online workbook.

The workbook is a valuable tool. To get the most out of this book, we highly recommend that you download the workbook now at www.fiveminuterelationshiprepair.com.

Chapter One

The Alarm That Hijacks Your Love

"I'LL BE HOME LATE. Go ahead and have dinner without me."

After hearing these words from her husband, Donna sat down and began to cry. "Eric's such a workaholic," she thought. "So busy all the time. And so tired. He never wants to talk or be intimate. What am I doing in this marriage?"

Donna was having another one of her inner conversations. She knew she should be having this conversation with Eric, but she feared Eric would just tune her out or be too distracted to listen. She thought, "I have to totally blow up if I want his attention. And that doesn't really get me what I want. I don't know what to do."

Two hours later, Eric walked into the house carrying an armful of papers and books. Before he could get to his desk to put his papers down, Donna called out from the kitchen, "Well, it's about time! What took so long?"

"Oh no," Eric thought to himself, "I hardly get through the front door, and she starts in on me. I should have stayed at the office. She never appreciates how hard I work to support this lifestyle she enjoys. She has no idea what I'm up against."

Eric and Donna were at it again. Only a few years into their marriage, they were already feeling disappointed and disconnected.

What causes such disconnection? We search for reasons — most of which involve blaming the other person: "If only he would pay more attention to me…" "If only she would be happy with what I do for her and stop finding fault…" Typically, we never get to the root of our distress.

We cannot see the real causes of emotional upsets and communication breakdowns because they are driven by a part of the brain that operates outside of conscious awareness. It acts like an alarm going off in the nervous system whenever it detects a potential threat to our survival, including a disturbance in our connection to "the one we depend on." In this book, we refer to this as the *survival alarm*.

Like radar, your survival alarm is always scanning for danger. As with other animals, this alarm system was built into the human species to quickly accelerate our bodies into action if a predatory animal was even suspected to be nearby. It prompts a fight-or-flight response, which in prehistoric times would have prevented us from being eaten by saber-toothed tigers!

Modern civilization has made our physical survival more secure, but the human brain still retains this primitive warning system. Nowadays, it mainly seems to be hooked up to how safe and secure we feel with an intimate partner. Things like a sharp voice tone or a disapproving facial expression can trigger an automatic impulse to attack or run for our lives, as if a tiger has suddenly appeared.

When Eric and Donna tried to make sense of why the romantic feelings they used to share seemed to have become so infrequent, it did not occur to them to look into the inner workings of their nervous systems. Like most people, they had learned to seek answers through the logic of their own limited understanding: Eric would wonder, "Can't she learn to speak to me without that critical edge in her voice? She knows this irritates me." Donna would ask herself, "Doesn't he know by now that all I need is a little more quality time with him? I'm not trying to control his life."

Perhaps you have been in Eric's or Donna's shoes in a significant love relationship — perhaps more than once. Maybe you can remember that awful sinking feeling of loss — when you find yourself thinking, "This is not the person I fell in love with. What is happening to us?"

Eric and Donna started out very much in love. They knew that not all couples make it and that about half of all marriages end in divorce. But they felt confident that their love was true and deep and strong. They weren't exactly youngsters when they met, either — which they considered another factor in favor of success. They had both been around and seen a lot of life. They knew themselves, or so they thought. But over time, as Eric tried to keep the peace and Donna tried to get more of his attention, they began to feel as if they were pulling in opposite directions.

Let's take a closer look at how these two lovers — who are composite characters we will revisit throughout the book — came to feel less and less safe in their relationship. Donna and Eric are based on hundreds of couples we've worked with. Their reactive incidents, and increasing inability to repair them on their own, are typical.

Eric and Donna's Fall from Grace

Donna was initially attracted to Eric's self-assured competence. He was the kind of guy who always knew how to make things work and how to fix them if they didn't. He mastered any technology that came along. As a successful architect, he could do any home-improvement job and even build a house from the ground up.

He had a confident gait and an inviting smile. But what really attracted Donna was his humility. Accustomed to guys who endlessly bragged about achievements and possessions, Donna almost had to drag out of Eric that he was a partner in a prestigious architectural firm. She also loved the deeply peaceful feeling she got around Eric, which was a natural counterbalance to her sometimes frenzied pace. She was calmed by his quiet demeanor and amazed at how intently he listened to her.

What attracted Eric to Donna was her colorful, expressive style. He loved the artistic way she dressed and her animated style of speaking and moving. Her expansive gestures, the way her eyes sparkled, the happy tone of her voice, and how she touched him, all turned him on in a big way. Donna's ready enthusiasm about even the smallest things was contagious and could lift Eric's spirits.

It didn't take long before they each felt they had found "the one." With Donna at his side, even a trip to the neighborhood coffeehouse seemed to Eric like a visit to some magnificent and unfamiliar place. When Donna had Eric by her side, she felt deeply safe and secure for the first time in her life. Together, life seemed full of magic and wonder. They were alive with excitement, curiosity, and hope. They wanted to share every possible moment with each other.

The pair experienced their first noteworthy upset about three months into their relationship. Eric arrived at Donna's house to take her out for a romantic evening. He arrived with dreams of sharing a pleasurable meal at their favorite café, followed by even more pleasurable lovemaking later on.

Shortly after arriving at Donna's home, Eric noticed that she seemed a bit tense. When he asked her what was wrong, she started recounting how her boss had unfairly overloaded her with work that afternoon.

As he tried to give her helpful advice on the situation, Donna seemed to get more distressed, rather than calming down. Desperate to keep his dream of a pleasurable evening intact, Eric responded by getting more logical about how she could solve her work problem, while his voice shifted to a lower, flatter, slightly impatient tone.

Suddenly, Donna shot back, "You think I'm stupid? I know all that! Why can't you see things my way once in a while?"

Eric was stunned. He didn't know what to say. All he could think of was, "I have to get out of here!" Without pausing, he stood up, walked down the stairs of her porch, and got back in his car, leaving Donna by herself in tears. Their date was cut short, and the honeymoon phase of their relationship came to an abrupt end.

Neither could make sense of what had happened. All they knew was that they each felt misunderstood and frustrated.

Identifying Triggers

Eric's behavior was received very differently from the way he intended. He had offered what he considered helpful input, but Donna got upset. For her, this happened quite automatically. She wasn't aware of why his words upset her so much.

Dissecting this interaction, we see that what initially provoked Donna was a shift in Eric's voice tone. It was like this pushed a button inside her unconscious mind, and she reacted. In other words, Donna was *triggered*. A certain stimulus — in this case, Eric's vocal tone and perhaps his facial expression — triggered her survival alarm. Of course, his words were not an actual threat to her survival, but the effect on her nervous system was pretty much the same as it would've been if a hungry tiger had appeared in the room.

Looking back over your own relationships, you can probably

recall times when your emotions seemed to take over, causing you to do and say things you would not have done had you not been triggered. This is because anything that threatens your felt sense of connection to the one you depend on — your significant other — can seem like a threat to your survival. When your survival alarm starts ringing, it pretty much takes over your nervous system.

Later, after calming down, Donna realized that Eric's tone of voice reminded her of how her father sounded when she was a child. She disclosed to Eric: "My father had a certain lecturing tone when I did things he disapproved of. When he spoke to me that way, I felt ridiculed and belittled. I would end up feeling like I wasn't good enough in his eyes. I never felt safe enough to tell him how much this hurt me."

Like most of us, Donna had an unhealed emotional wound from childhood. Early experiences with her father instilled in her an unconscious sensitivity to certain voice tones. Her alarm was set off by the way Eric sounded as he gave advice. We commonly call this "getting triggered" or "having one's buttons pushed." When this happens, we feel and react in ways that are often out of proportion to the actual situation.

Eric had no way of seeing into Donna's unconscious mind. It was certainly not his intention to belittle her. He thought he was being helpful. But he, too, had fear thoughts arise that remained unconscious and probably fueled his need to give advice using that flat voice tone. He was afraid that Donna's agitation over her boss might spoil their night together. He was unaware that his body, including his vocal cords, tightened up when he heard the person he loved in distress. He had a pattern of trying to fix things before they got out of control.

Both Donna and Eric had a lot going on inside of them that they had not learned to pay attention to. Without realizing it, their bodies and minds were overtaken by the survival states of fight, flight, or freeze.

Whenever Eric was triggered, his whole body would tense up, and his mind would either race with too many thoughts or he would want to do something — like running away. This is the *flight response*. When Donna was triggered, her stomach would get tight, and her breathing would become shallow. She would stop listening to the hurtful input and start using loud words to fend off the danger. This is the *fight response*.

A third common reaction is the *freeze response*, where someone starts to shut down, go blank, or numb out emotionally. Later, we will see how Eric gradually fell into this response as the couple's reactivity escalated over the years.

As Donna's alarm reacted to Eric's voice tone, it affected her own voice. The moment she heard his flat tone, her own voice shifted, becoming louder, higher pitched, and strident. Hearing Donna's voice increase in volume and tension, Eric's alarm got triggered. In childhood, Eric saw that bad things happened when people yelled. He had learned to be afraid of harsh voice tones and angry facial expressions. When he saw people getting angry, he would run and hide in his bedroom closet to protect himself. Now, when Donna's voice got louder and her face angry, he suddenly felt the need to escape.

As observers, we can see how Donna and Eric's survival alarms took over, quickly sending them into states of upset that completely overpowered their ability to communicate in a conscious or loving way.

All of us have suffered such upsets. Unhealed experiences from our past programmed our survival alarms to scan for similar cues in the present, and when our alarms go off, we are catapulted into offensive, defensive, or numbed-out reactions. When we get triggered like this, things can spiral rapidly out of control, even when circumstances otherwise seem normal and familiar. We fall under the influence of adrenaline or other strong body chemicals. When this happens, we don't realize how inebriated we are. Just like getting drunk, it can take time to discharge such biochemical states before our higher brain functions come back online.

Which Part of Your Brain Is Communicating?

In any given moment, your communication will be governed either by your higher brain or by your survival alarm. It's important to understand that you and your partner will feel and behave differently depending on which part of your brain is in charge.

The Higher Brain

Brain scientists have found that certain areas in the cortex — especially parts in the front and center — play a vital role in our highest human capacities for loving thoughts, feelings, and actions. The neocortex is that outer layer you see in photos of the whole brain. It is home to regions associated with conscious awareness. Central areas of the frontal lobes are involved in our abilities to be empathetic, to put ourselves in another person's shoes, and to understand what is going on inside someone.

This is the part of the brain that helps you see the complexity of an interpersonal situation, stay calm, comprehend and care about each other's needs, negotiate and collaborate, get creative, and ultimately arrive at a win-win solution. This brain functionality is essential for effective two-way communication. It provides a braking function, allowing you to patiently listen to your partner, pause as needed for comprehension, and move through a topic at an appropriate speed.

Neuroscientists are developing detailed maps of these brain areas, but for simplicity's sake we will call this the *higher brain*.

Essentially, a well-functioning higher brain is what you need if you want to behave in ways that maximize feelings of love and trust.

Operating from your higher brain, you are more likely to be viewed as a "friend" to your partner's brain. Your face will look friendly, your voice tone will sound friendly, and you will have friendlier things to say — even while ironing out differences. So if your goal is to work things out and make sure everyone feels heard, you want your higher brain to be in charge of the conversation.

The Survival Alarm

The survival alarm's prime directive is to keep you alive. A key component of this alarm system in the brain is the amygdala. The amygdala is buried deep in the middle of your brain — well below the cortical regions associated with conscious cognition. You cannot see this part in photos of the whole brain because it is hidden beneath the neocortex. How it operates and controls your state of mind is similarly hidden from your normal awareness. It continually scans for signs of safety or danger.

Since survival is its higher priority, if the alarm detects even the slightest sign of danger, it quickly takes control and changes your body chemistry to support immediate self-preservation. It's strictly a "shoot first, ask questions later" deal. The alarm reacts automatically, instinctively, and without your permission. Most of the time you don't even realize when your conversations have been taken over by this primitive part of your brain.

At high levels of activation, the survival alarm can dramatically hijack your higher brain, taking vital interpersonal functions offline. When triggered, the alarm has no concern with negotiating a mutually satisfying solution. It lacks the empathetic circuitry of the higher brain. It has no ability to understand another's needs. Remember, those higher brain functions operate too slowly to save you from a saber-toothed tiger! When survival is at stake, everything has to happen fast.

People are not at their best interpersonally when their survival alarm is triggered. The quick, knee-jerk reactions like fight, flight, or freeze cause people to yell, blow up, blame, try to be right, create distance, shut down, avoid, build walls, or get defensive. While your alarm is ringing, your braking capacity is absent, so things can easily accelerate out of control.

Operating from this part of the brain, you will be viewed as a "foe" to your partner's primitive brain. Your face will not look friendly, your voice tone may sound threatening, and the things you say will be met with suspicion or resistance.

If you recognize that you or your partner is in a triggered state, then you can take steps to get your higher brains back online. Realize how automatic this whole triggering process is — and stop blaming yourself or your partner for causing such upsets. Remember, your alarms take over without anyone's conscious awareness or permission. Nobody chooses to behave this way. In the next chapter, you will learn how to quickly stop an escalating situation so you do not continue to throw fuel on the fire. But first, let's look more deeply at what happens to couples who do not have these skills.

Spiraling into the Hole

Over time, if we do not repair upsets, we will find ourselves caught in a downward spiral. More and more often, we won't be able to stop ourselves from being pulled down into that unwanted, upsetting place we metaphorically call *the Hole*. Each time we have an unresolved upset, it will get progressively harder to dig ourselves out. Any single reactive incident will be compounded by all past unrepaired upsets. The Hole gets deeper each time we fall into it.

As we stumble into the Hole, some people react with aggressive pursuit, others with detached withdrawal. Others try to be reasonable and explain or defend themselves. In any of these states, we are incapable of feeling and expressing our tender needs and feelings. The fight-or-flight states alter body chemistry — arming us with what early humans needed to kill or escape a saber-toothed tiger. The state of freeze is how the nervous system numbs the body so we won't feel pain if the tiger has trapped us.

When the survival alarm takes over, our words may get dramatic in an attempt to feel powerful or get attention. We generalize, instead of focusing on what actually happened. For instance, Donna might accuse, "You *never* help around here! You *only* think about yourself." And Eric might shoot back, "You're *always* complaining! *Nothing* I do is *ever* good enough for you!"

Lost in fight-flight-freeze, we lose our ability to really hear and understand one another — although we are convinced we are still having a useful dialogue. When we're in the Hole, the other person appears like a caricature — with features exaggerated in the worst ways. We don't see the real person because we're looking through the lens of our fears. We have lost the higher brain's refined capacities to see complexity, so we see one another through the lens of our stories and stereotypes.

In the Hole, our ability to reassure each other and resolve issues is disabled. Yet, despite our reduced mental capacities, we keep working the situation. We keep digging ourselves deeper into the Hole, as if there were gold down there. Each person tries to get in that last word. Emotions escalate. Sometimes someone will pull out their big guns and threaten to end the relationship — triggering even higher states of alarm.

It is sad that partners tend to blame each other for these

upsets. Neither can see how he or she is contributing to the escalation and mutual distress. We forget that there is no real choice involved for either party. Both people's higher brains have been hijacked by their survival alarms, and both are reacting as if they are fighting for their lives.

Donna and Eric Dig Their Hole More Deeply

After Donna and Eric got married, the reactive pattern they first experienced when they were dating grew more frequent and intense. Neither understood how to resolve these upsetting events when they occurred. It was almost as if each was increasingly looking for reasons to get upset. This came to a head one night when they were sitting on the couch watching a movie. About halfway through, Eric began to feel restless. Without saying anything, he got up and left to find a snack in the kitchen.

As Eric got up and walked away, Donna felt her gut tighten. A story came up in her mind that went like this: "We planned to spend the evening together. And now he's just going off by himself — as if I don't exist. He never considers *my* feelings. He always just does whatever *he* wants." Hearing Eric rummaging around in the refrigerator, seemingly oblivious to her, she felt heat rise in her face and head. Finally, she could not contain her upset. Without getting off the couch, she called out to him, "Don't mind me. I just occupy space around here. Obviously, you're in your own world — as usual!"

Hearing Donna's strident tone, Eric froze. He felt shocked — caught completely off guard. He stopped looking for something to eat and for a minute just stared into space, trying to get himself ready to go back into the living room and face Donna. This gave Donna time to shoot out a few more zingers: "We never want to do the same things. We can't even agree on a movie. I knew you didn't really want to watch this with me, but you just say 'yes' even when you don't mean it. How can I ever trust you to tell me the truth?"

Finally, Eric entered the living room and, trying to sound reasonable, said, "I don't think there is anything wrong with getting up for a minute to get myself something to eat. That's all I did."

Donna detected a superior tone in Eric's response — something she was hearing more frequently — and this upset her even more. She shot back, "So you're the big authority on matters of the heart, eh? Your heart is *shut down*, Eric. You're just a walking, talking machine. Big and smart, but without a heart. Why can't you ever see things from *my* side? Why can't you ever think of anyone but yourself?"

Still frozen inside, Eric continued to reason with Donna: "I didn't do anything against you. Honestly, I was hungry. I could see where the movie was going, and I thought that might be a good time to take a little food break."

Donna became frustrated by Eric's coolness and defensiveness — that flat, superior, dismissive tone — and so she turned up the volume in a desperate attempt to pull some emotion from him: "A little food break? I can't believe you. We decided *together* to watch this movie. I actually thought we were going to have a nice evening together for a change. You've been ignoring me and ignoring my needs for months. You are like *ice*. You can't just walk away when we're doing things together. It's not what couples do — *if they care*. You obviously do not care about anyone but yourself."

Eric felt a familiar tightness in his throat that made it difficult for him to speak. Feeling helpless, he walked out of the living room and went down the hall into his study. There, he shut the door and turned on his computer as his mind flooded with thoughts: "This is hopeless. I'll never find a way to get through to her. I'm not a fighter. I just want peace. I'm *not* going to engage in this kind of argument. This is beneath me. Donna calls me superior. Well, I *am* superior to her in how I deal with things like this. She just goes nuts on me." As an escape from their argument, Eric immersed himself in a work project, telling himself he didn't really care what Donna did or said. He would simply refuse to respond. That's how he had been dealing with his growing sense of powerlessness and frustration.

Now feeling panicked, Donna got up and marched down the hall, yelling, "You think you can just shut me up by walking out! You are totally and completely insensitive. You suck as a husband. I am so patient with you and your busy schedule. But it never changes. And it will never change, Eric. You need to get your head out of your ass, and keep it out!" With these words, Donna started sobbing loudly right outside Eric's office door.

"Now she's going to manipulate me with her tears," Eric thought. "Thank God, she's not breaking down the door. I can't stand all this drama. I never wanted this type of relationship. We used to get along so great. What happened?"

Still sobbing, Donna finally collapsed onto the floor, but after crying for another minute, a wave of determination came over her. She thought: "I've gotten way too dependent on Eric. I need to start thinking more about myself and my needs. He, for sure, will never meet my needs. So I'll just go shopping and get myself something nice. I can be too busy, too — just like he always is." When Donna realized it was too late to go to the mall, she went back into the living room and tried to get reinterested in the movie.

As Donna sat alone, her mind raced. She considered knocking on Eric's door one more time or perhaps texting him, and she rehearsed in her mind all the things she wanted to say. She felt right and justified: "When people love each other, they don't just get up and leave the room like that. That is insensitive. That shows a lack of feeling. Can't he see this?"

In his study, Eric, too, was building his case: "Donna always goes to the worst-case scenario. And she won't listen to reason. That whole thing was completely unnecessary. Can't she see how she ruined a perfectly nice evening with her paranoia? Why can't she see the big picture?"

This incident shows some of the typical ways couples try to be heard and understood during a communication breakdown. Both partners hate arguing. They hate the feeling of distance. But they just keep doing what they have always done — criticizing, pursuing, provoking, distancing, hiding out, labeling, judging, and trying to be right. Their survival alarms have pulled them into the Hole.

We can probably all relate to Donna and Eric's pain. We can see they are both trying to be heard. But they cannot hear each other's real needs because they are caught in a downward spiral. Perhaps we can see what might work better, or perhaps we even recognize ourselves in parts of their story.

Resolution Is Impossible in the Hole

No matter how hard you work at being understood, if you're trying to communicate while in the Hole, you will only make matters worse. Your only tool is a shovel, and anything you do will just dig you in deeper. What's Rule No. 1 when you find yourself in the Hole? *Stop digging!*

There are many types of shovels couples use to dig themselves further into the Hole. Engaging in any of the following behaviors will sabotage your attempts to be heard:

- ❖ blaming
- ❖ criticizing

- ❖ name-calling
- ❖ judging
- ❖ attacking
- ❖ prodding
- ❖ pursuing
- ❖ provoking
- ❖ getting defensive
- ❖ withdrawing
- ❖ shutting down
- ❖ proving you're right
- ❖ trying to win

These reactive behaviors are signs that your higher brain has gotten hijacked. Directed by the instinctive attack-defend part of the brain, they are really attempts to protect oneself. Read this list again, and think about which ones you tend to use when you're upset. Are you aware of what happens in your body when you are in such states? Have you ever tried to stop yourself in the middle of one of these trips to the Hole? If you have tried to stop, you know how hard this can be. You want to resolve the upset and get back to feeling safe and happy together. But something beyond your control seems to take over.

To get a sense of the power of our automatic patterns, imagine that you and your partner are discussing a sensitive topic (such as sex, money, or your kids). Suddenly, all the smoke alarms in your house start blaring so loud you can't even follow your own thinking, much less hear your partner accurately. Your system is flooded. Do you think you'll be able to successfully resolve an interpersonal issue while all your alarms are blaring?

Only after all of the alarms stop ringing can we discuss a sensitive topic with any hope of finding a good solution. That's impossible to do while being overtaken by the urgent impulses to flee for one's life, to desperately fight for it, or to numb out if both of those options seem hopeless. So, if you have ever felt hopeless in trying to stop your downward spiral, give yourself some compassion. This happens to everyone. States of fight, flight, and freeze are human biological imperatives that get executed automatically by a part of the brain we cannot control.

What if we had stopped Donna in the middle of her angry outburst and asked, "Do you think you're in physical danger right now?" She wouldn't have thought so. Nor would she have realized her body was in a state of fight-or-flight, rushing energy into her limbs while shutting down her higher brain capacities. Like most of us, Donna had no idea that her survival alarm was ringing.

What if we had asked her, "Do you think the upset you are feeling is entirely about Eric? Do you have any awareness right now about how your father used to speak to you in a superior tone?" Since she was wrapped up in blaming Eric, it's unlikely that she was thinking about her father at all. However, she had made this connection at least once before, so our reminder might have given her pause.

Or we could have asked her, "What sensations do you notice in your body right now?" If directed to observe this, she might have reported feeling a knot in her stomach or a shaky feeling in her chest. By paying close attention to sensations in the body — especially in the chest and belly — we can detect when our survival alarm has gone off.

When we fall into a state of fight, flight, or freeze, we usually think our upset feelings are the result of the other person's behavior. Sometimes we even think a partner is choosing to trigger us. We have no idea what old programming lies at the root of our triggers.

Why the Alarm Mistakes One's Partner for a Tiger

Vocal tone, facial expression, and physical gestures are continually being read by our survival alarms as we interact with others. Some signals are inherently triggering. A female's high, shrill voice is how our earliest human ancestors signaled distress to get others to run for safety. A male projecting a low, booming tone is how men scared away a predator. Someone showing teeth or sneering in anger can activate a partner's alarm. Sudden physical gestures imply threat. Behaviors like these will reflexively trigger our alarms.

Of course, a great number of our triggers are programmed by past experiences that were scary, painful, or upsetting. This was true for Donna when Eric's advice-giving voice resembled a tonal quality her father used in her childhood. Eric unwittingly pushed an old button wired into her alarm. Simultaneously, as Donna reacted, her angry tone triggered in Eric the threat he felt in childhood when his parents started yelling. This is how Donna and Eric unintentionally cotriggered false alarms in each other's survival systems. Their alarms did not distinguish that these sounds were now coming from different people in an entirely different time and place.

Our alarm systems are built to make mistakes. A good alarm, by its very nature, will overgeneralize and sound a lot of false alarms. It's about survival, after all. Hence, our alarms go off automatically if an intimate partner does something even remotely similar to earlier painful or scary experiences.

Core Needs for Emotional Safety in an Intimate Partnership

In an intimate partnership we need to feel emotionally safe and secure. Otherwise we will be triggered to some degree. We want to feel like we have each other's backs, operate like a team, and can rely on each other. We want to trust that we are accepted, valued, and loved and that we can be our authentic selves in the relationship.

What got Donna's alarm ringing wasn't a threat to physical survival but rather a threat to her feeling safely connected emotionally with Eric. In her mind, her need to feel valued and respected had been threatened. When she heard his voice, she was flooded with old, unprocessed painful memories about her dad. When her dad used that tone, she thought he was saying she wasn't smart. Feeling small and inadequate, she'd sometimes run to her room and cry. As an adult, Donna's alarm mistakenly thought Eric was putting her down. This explains why she suddenly yelled, "You think I'm stupid?" Her old fear button of not being good enough got triggered.

Within an intimate partnership we all need to feel valued and respected. These are core emotional needs. Couples therapist Sue Johnson says our core needs are like air, food, and water in our love lives. To feel safe and secure with a partner, we need to feel these needs are met. If we feel any are not met, our survival alarms will instinctively react.

If we were to state our *core needs* to a partner, we might say something like this:

> **I need to feel…** connected to you, accepted by you, valued by you, appreciated by you, respected by you, needed by you, that you care about me, that I matter to you, that we are a team, that I can count on you, that I can reach out for you, that you'll comfort me if I'm in distress, that you'll be there if I need you.

Take a moment to reflect on your own life. Think about an incident that occurred in an intimate relationship that upset you.

Maybe you got angry, felt hurt, or shut down. Now, look at the list of core needs above. Which ones seemed to be threatened at that moment?

If one of these needs feels like it is not being met, you won't feel safe, your alarm will ring as if it's a matter of survival, and you may get triggered into a state of fight, flight, or freeze. A *core fear* is being triggered, and you will react protectively.

Core Fears Trigger Reactive Behaviors

Core needs and fears are like two sides of a coin. If a core need feels frustrated or unmet, a core fear will be triggered. For example, if you don't feel accepted or valued, this will likely trigger a core fear of being inadequate or a failure to your mate.

We are especially vulnerable to such triggers in our intimate partnerships. Even though Eric feels quite confident in his career and with his buddies, when Donna complains, his fear of being inadequate can get triggered. Similarly, nobody triggers Donna's insecurities the way Eric does with his lecturing tone.

Like Donna and Eric, we all react when core fears get triggered. We attempt to avoid reexperiencing as adults what we found too painful, scary, or overwhelming as children. We instinctively protect ourselves with reactions like arguing or walking away. Reactive behaviors help us feel more in control. Instead of letting ourselves feel the emotional pain resulting from a distressing incident, a reactive feeling momentarily helps us feel big and righteous rather than small and powerless.

Here are examples of core fears that get triggered in adult relationships. Which of these have you felt in a significant love relationship?

❖ **Fear of being abandoned:** You fear your partner might leave. You feel that your partner doesn't need you as much as you need him or her.

❖ **Fear of being unimportant or invisible:** You fear you are not as important to your partner as other things or people, or that you don't really matter.

❖ **Fear of being rejected:** You have trouble feeling accepted or valued just the way you are. You fear that you, or your needs, will be rejected.

❖ **Fear of being inadequate or a failure:** Complaints or criticisms trigger fears that you are not good enough, that you are inadequate or unlovable.

❖ **Fear of being blamed:** You fear being seen as wrong or as the cause of relationship upsets, so you either defend yourself or shut down in the face of negative feedback.

❖ **Fear of being controlled:** You fear feeling weak or vulnerable. You instinctively try to be in charge or control of any situation.

❖ **Fear of being trapped or suffocated:** You fear intrusion, losing yourself, or being consumed by others. You become uncomfortable with others' expectations or too much closeness.

A core fear promotes an unconscious state of vigilance. You become hypersensitive to cues that the feared event may be about to happen. Your perception gets distorted; it becomes biased toward noticing even the tiniest similarity to past events, thus increasing the likelihood that your survival alarm will soon be ringing.

Trading in IQ Points for Limb Strength

When you are triggered into fight or flight, your heart races. Your lungs attempt to pull in more oxygen. Adrenaline starts pumping. Other systems shut down, like digestion and saliva production, so that the energy they consume can all be put into immediate survival activities.

The states of fight or flight have one basic biological purpose — to provide maximum strength and energy to your limbs, giving you the power to run faster and get away or to fight harder and win. Basically, you are cashing in IQ points for limb strength. A mother can lift a car off her baby with such strength! But an intimate couple will find no benefit from brute strength when trying to resolve interpersonal issues. That type of strength only serves to dig you deeper into the Hole.

The freeze state is a kind of self-anesthesia administered by the nervous system to numb you from feeling a painful, overwhelming, and likely fatal physical attack. It's like going into shock. You space out or shut down. This is useful if your alarm concludes that a tiger is about to kill you. It enables you to avoid feeling intense physical pain. But again, it is not helpful to a couple trying to resolve an issue.

We've all seen how drinking too much alcohol can distort thinking and impair abilities. The same goes for adrenaline or anesthesia. When we get triggered, we are essentially operating under the influence of powerful chemicals. But there are no empty shot glasses lined up on a bar in front of us. Instead, a whole lot of juice is being served up by internal bartenders, and, blindsided, we are suddenly inebriated without realizing it. With diminished brain capacities, we suffer black-and-white thinking, tunnel vision, or simply going blank. Stuck in attack-defend mode, we may numb out or say things we later regret. And later, we are unable to accurately recall what happened.

When Donna was activated, her voice would get louder, faster, and shriller. She would frequently interrupt or dominate the conversation, as if being driven by an urgent need to accelerate. You could sense the adrenaline in the volume and rapid speed of her words.

Eric's tendency was to freeze. His vocal tone would get flatter, and it would eventually trail off. His words would become more sparse, with long pauses. His mind might go blank and words escape him. You could sense the anesthesia of shock reducing his ability to speak.

With their diminished capacities, it never occurred to Donna or Eric to stop reacting and, instead, to reassure each other they were actually safe. They didn't even realize that they were triggered.

It would be great if we could realize when we are getting triggered. But body chemistry is a powerful intoxicant. As people do in twelve-step meetings like AA, we might want to admit that we are powerless over adrenaline (or anesthesia), and that our communication has become unmanageable.

Warning Signs of a Survival Alarm Takeover

What can you do when your alarm starts ringing? Step one is to accept that this sort of thing happens — even to the nicest, most intelligent, and most conscious people. Step two is learning how to recognize the early warning signs of being triggered.

Paying attention to your body sensations will help you recognize when your survival alarm has been activated. While we don't have any direct control over getting triggered, we can learn to do something different once we realize our alarms are activated. The first signs are in the physical body.

What do you feel in your body when you become upset? You might feel a knot in your stomach, pressure in your chest, or a lump in your throat. You might feel your heart pounding, a shaky or fluttering feeling, or a churning in your gut. Some people feel a tightness in their muscles, shoulders, or chest, while others feel heat rise as their body temperature changes. These are typical signs of fight or flight. Signs of freeze might include feeling fuzzy, lethargic, shut down, drained, a loss of energy, a slumping over, a sense of numbness, or going blank.

Which "F" Overtakes Your Higher Brain?

Some peoples' nervous systems automatically react by going into fight. When triggered, they tend to get frustrated or angry. This often manifests as some form of complaining, prodding, blowing up, or in some other way going on the attack. Others tend to flee. Driven by anxiety or fear, they may withdraw, distance themselves, or leave. Still others fall into a freeze state — feeling confused, shutting down, numbing out, getting paralyzed, or not knowing what to say or do.

Our nervous system will favor one of these Fs, but they are all available. Another F will be used if the first one doesn't work. Someone may initially get triggered into a state of fight, but if that doesn't work, they will flee, and then as a last resort, freeze. Another person's nervous system may initially provoke a flight reaction, but if that's not possible, they will fight.

Some partners react in similar ways. Both blow up or both shut down. Many partners differ. One goes into the state of fight, pursuing the other like a cheetah chasing a gazelle — while the other flees or freezes.

A very common relationship dynamic is between a pursuer and a withdrawer. We see this in Donna and Eric's relationship. Donna acts like a pursuer — complaining, criticizing, prodding, pushing, blowing up. The F that takes her over is fight. Her reactive feelings are frustration and anger. Eric is a withdrawer. The F taking him over can be flight or freeze. He often begins by ignoring, distancing himself, staying in his head, pushing feelings away, or shutting down. Then, he may feel nervous and anxious or confused and numb. Finally, he might walk away.

Over a long time period, the F that we go to first might change. Someone who initially shuts down around angry yelling may eventually start blowing up, too. Or someone who pursues and prods may burn out and start building walls and creating distance. What is your dominant F in a relationship? Have you tended to be a frustrated pursuer or a shut-down withdrawer? Does this depend on your partner's style?

Look at the following list, which groups reactive feelings into three categories of fight, flight, and freeze. The six words in each category can be thought of as different intensities of each state. Put a check next to any reactive feelings you experience in your relationship (present or past).

We recommend you do this exercise in the free online workbook, which is in the "Reactive Feelings" section (available at www.fiveminuterelationshiprepair.com). You will refer back to this list later.

Fight
- ❏ annoyed
- ❏ irritated
- ❏ frustrated
- ❏ angry
- ❏ resentful
- ❏ infuriated

Flight
- ❏ nervous
- ❏ worried
- ❏ insecure
- ❏ anxious

- ❏ fearful
- ❏ panicked

Freeze
- ❏ hopeless
- ❏ confused
- ❏ ashamed
- ❏ stuck
- ❏ numb
- ❏ paralyzed

In the next chapter, you will learn what to do when you notice one of these Fs wreaking havoc in your relationship.

Chapter Two

Install a Pause Button

WHAT DO YOU DO IF YOU NOTICE you or your partner in one of these F states? How can you get your higher brain functioning again after your survival alarm has been triggered?

You need to ask for a pause, as in, "Can we pause for a moment? I can't think straight." Do not keep trying to be heard. Any attempt to resolve an issue when you or your partner is triggered is like trying to put out a fire with gasoline. You'll do more damage than good because the part of your brain designed for battle and survival has taken over. You will be communicating without the higher brain power you need to resolve things.

Whenever you realize someone has been triggered, it's important to find a way to stop and calm yourselves. Find your brakes — or develop some. *Brakes* is a metaphor to describe how your higher brain can stop an accelerating state of alarm. When your survival alarm is triggered, it's just like pressing the accelerator on a car; your heart speeds up and pumps massive amounts of energy into your limbs for battle or escape. The braking function of your nervous system can slow down your heart rate and quiet your nervous system so you're calm enough to communicate productively.

Having good brakes means that you recognize when you or your partner is triggered and slow everything down until your higher brains can get back in charge. Then you'll be able to consider what each other is saying. With good brakes, each of you can resist the impulse to interrupt the other or prove your point. Once your higher brains are back online, you realize that you are safe; the issue between you is not a threat to your survival.

Even if you tend to go quickly into a triggered state, you can learn to develop a better braking system. First, become curious about the ways you and your partner go on automatic. This way, you can become more aware of the signs when someone is triggered. Then, let go of any shame you might have about the fact that you sometimes overreact. Remember that everyone has triggers, and everyone has unfinished business from the past.

Consider making an agreement with your partner that either person can ask for a pause whenever one of you feels activated. Each time you do this, you give time for your rational minds to reassure your triggered minds that you are actually safe. You give time for your nervous systems to calm down. These conscious efforts will increase your capacity to brake more quickly at signs of distress. Over time, reactive incidents will decrease.

Whenever you realize you or your partner are triggered, here are some ways to initiate a pause. You can say something like:

"I need to pause."
"Can we slow down for a moment?"
"Our reactive pattern is happening."
"I'm getting triggered."
"Let's take a break."

The point of pausing is to insert a new choice into what is otherwise an automatic accelerating sequence of reactive behaviors. You are learning to interrupt an unconscious pattern. At first, you may not be entirely successful in your attempts to pause, but at least you are consciously recognizing the need to do so. No matter when it dawns on you that one of you is triggered, ask for a pause.

Saying "I need to pause" is like giving a short signal. If your higher brain wasn't in the very process of being taken offline, you might be able to offer a more complete statement. For instance, you might be able to say: "I am triggered, and reactivity is taking over our communication. My higher brain is getting hijacked, and I can't even really hear you, much less give you the response you need. I'd like to return to this conversation after we take some time to calm our survival alarms. I am committed to finding a solution, and I want to do this together. But first I need to pause and calm down. Won't you please join me?"

Create a Pause Signal

Typically, when you're triggered, you won't be able to say those reassuring words. You simply don't have enough higher brain power when your survival alarm kicks in. So it works best to agree on a signal that will be easy to remember and easy to hear, such as, "I need to pause," "Time out," or "I'm triggered." It's good to discuss these options with your partner and agree on a pause signal ahead of time.

Make it short and simple. Use a signal that will be distinct and obvious even when you have lost 90 percent of your IQ points.

Whatever you choose, do not say, "*You* need to pause," or "I see that *you* are getting triggered." If you want your partner to feel safe with you, stay on your own side of the net. Speak only about your own feelings and needs.

How Long Do You Pause?

The length of time you need to pause will vary. It depends on how quickly you can calm your nervous systems and return to feeling safe. You will learn tools for calming in the next chapter. It is easier to calm yourself if you can call for a pause before your activation levels have gotten too high. The more quickly you recognize that you or your partner is triggered, the more quickly you can recover.

Ideally, the moment you notice your familiar reactive feelings (such as anger), your reactive stories (such as, "He doesn't respect me"), or body sensations (such as jaw tension), immediately ask for a pause. When you spot reactivity quickly, you may only need a moment of silence to calm down. But if you both reach higher levels of activation, you may need to pause for much longer, perhaps half an hour or more.

When someone gives a pause signal, immediately stop talking and take a minute in silence. Reflect on how upset you are, and do what you can to calm down. Then briefly decide when to come back together to repair any damage and reassure any fears that arose. Aim to keep this pause fairly short, or as short as possible, but if you find the break is too short, and you're still not calm, then ask for more time. The first step in any relationship repair is developing the ability to pause and calm yourself.

Research shows that if couples continue talking about an issue before they calm down and soothe themselves, they will escalate to even higher levels of fight-or-flight mode, where even more damage gets done. Your nervous system needs adequate time to discharge the body state of being activated. On average, it can take twenty to thirty minutes for the higher brain to get back in charge if you have become really triggered.

If one of you takes longer to calm down than the other, then wait until you are both ready. You can only repair the damage together. One thing that helps is to remember that, when your alarm is ringing, it is undoubtedly a false alarm. Reminding yourself of this can help you calm yourself more quickly. Then, if you find you get calm before your partner, you might offer reassurance, saying something like, "I'm sorry this is happening," "I love you," "We're okay," or "We'll get through this." Simple reassurances can go a long way toward reducing activation levels and make repair easier.

Never attempt to resolve an issue until you both have had time to calm your nervous systems. Also, pausing should never be used as a way to avoid an issue. Beware of the tendency to use your pause agreement as a way to put off dealing with the issue. Generally, it is not in anybody's best interest to delay repair — because the longer you delay, the more the upset will grow and get transferred into long-term memory structures in the brain. This will generalize the upset and make triggering even more likely in the future.

Ingredients of an Effective Pause Agreement

To make pausing an effective tool, it helps to have a formal agreement with your partner. This can be a verbal agreement, or you could write up a contract that you both sign. See "A Formal Pause Agreement," page 41, for a sample.

Your agreement should contain the following ingredients:

You Choose a Pause Signal

Pick a verbal pause signal that feels right to both partners. It should be short and clearly identifiable in any context. Examples: "I need to pause." "I need a time out." "I'm getting triggered." "Our cycle is happening." "Let's take a break." "Whoa!" "Can we slow down for a moment?" You will use these words only and leave it at that. You will not slip in phrases that justify your actions or imply blame. You will not ask for a pause and then interject some choice last words (like, "I need a time out from your complaining").

Either of You Can Initiate It

You both agree to be responsible for initiating the pause signal whenever you notice reactivity in either party. You agree to learn to recognize the signs whenever you or your partner are in a state of distress — characteristic sensations in your body, recurring reactive stories, certain looks on your partner's face, or tones of voice.

You Both Agree to Pause

You agree that, whenever your pause signal is given by either partner, you will both stop talking about the matter at hand. Things will immediately come to a halt. No explanation is needed. You will simply stop whatever you're talking about and pause.

You Determine the Pause Length

Once someone gives the pause signal, you will immediately be silent for a brief time to reflect on how triggered you are and how long you'll probably need to calm down. Is a minute or two sufficient? Or will you need an hour or more to calm down? Can you continue being together, or do you need to spend time apart? Agree on when you will get back together to repair the reactive incident.

You Reassure Each Other before the Pause

Whenever you are able, it is helpful to offer some brief reassurance to your partner before taking a break. Offer supportive touch, a hug, or a short reassuring message like, "We're okay. We can re-pair this together." This can begin to calm your nervous systems. Such reassurances are extremely important in those cases where you or your partner feel the need to physically separate in order to calm down. This will go a long way to prevent a sense of abandonment, rejection, or other similar buttons from getting pushed during the period you are apart.

You Calm Down during the Pause

During the pause it's your job to calm down and get your full brain power back. Chapters 3, 14, and 15 give specific tools to calm your nervous system and work with the feelings that have been triggered. Knowing how to use these tools will give you confidence that you do not have to avoid difficult issues.

You Repair Together after the Pause

After returning from your pause, whether it's a minute or an hour, you agree to engage together in the Five-Minute Relationship Repair process, where you look together at what just happened and share what you discovered about yourself during your pause. This process is described in chapter 10.

Your Personal Reason to Pause

When you say, "I need to pause," you are really telling your own triggered survival alarm and your own reactive behaviors to pause. You are developing stronger brakes in your brain that will keep your mind from accelerating out of control. This is a way to take better care of yourself. Whether or not your partner is able to join you in your attempts to halt an argument, you still owe it to yourself to stop acting out your part of a reactive pattern.

Sometimes this may mean taking a pause and being silent

without your partner's consent — or even leaving the room if necessary. If you genuinely need a break, you can always excuse yourself to use the bathroom. But don't walk away abruptly. Tell your partner you are taking a break to center yourself. Be sure to add that once you calm down, you will come back to talk things out. If possible, tell your partner how long you need. Five minutes can often do the job.

Use It or Lose It

Even after making a formal agreement, most people still hesitate or forget to use their pause signal at first. Many people just can't admit they are triggered. They may carry too much shame about this. They see it as a sign of weakness to admit they are too activated to think clearly. Others are afraid they might insult their partner or further rock the boat. Many resist calling for a pause because it triggers a sense of disconnection or abandonment. They are afraid to stop talking because talking helps them feel connected — even though, in reality, they are making matters worse.

Mainly, though, we go on automatic and don't even notice we need to pause. Most of us have learned to tolerate our habitual reactive patterns. We don't even realize how often we are triggered. Using a pause signal requires a fairly high level of self-awareness. The tools offered here will help you become more aware in each moment about your reactive feelings and thoughts.

Think of it this way: you and your partner are in the activation-management business. It is *your* job to give your agreed-upon pause signal as soon as you sense even the slightest reactivity in your communication. Give your signal whenever you notice any early warning signs that you or your partner is beginning to get activated.

Partners often have a hard time stopping when their survival alarms have prepared them for battle. It can be difficult to stop in the midst of such powerful feelings. If you are the one asking for a pause, don't give up if your partner keeps talking. Simply repeat your special signal — in a soft or neutral tone of voice. If nothing else works, take a bathroom break (or the equivalent) to create a pause.

Make Pausing a Daily Practice

The best way to ensure success using the pause tool is to practice using it often — even when you are only slightly uncomfortable or in situations where you are not highly activated. For example, if your partner is talking too fast for you to understand, you could ask for a pause. During your pause, you would each reflect on what you were feeling as words began to fly around faster. Then, you would come back together and talk about what you each saw or learned about yourselves. Or try using a practice pause if you start losing track, or if one of you is interrupting the other person.

By putting your pause signal into practice in your ordinary conversations, you will begin building a supportive new habit. Its repeated use will make the signal easier for each of you to say and hear, thereby increasing the likelihood that you'll remember to use the tool when you really need it. And consider this. Partners who make a regular habit of pausing during conversations — stopping a moment here and there and putting more breathing room into their dialogue — tend to hear and respond to each other better. This alone can prevent accidental triggering, which is often a product of going too fast without "checking in" with yourself to get present.

Donna and Eric Use the Pause Tool

Over time, Donna and Eric's relationship suffered increasing amounts of upset as one unrepaired incident built upon another.

About a month before their twelfth anniversary, they realized how out of proportion their reactions had become to actual events. What might have been a minor tiff years ago could now sometimes throw them off for days. In a rare moment of putting blame aside, they admitted to each other how they *both* had to learn to communicate better or they might soon reach a point of no return.

One of the first things they learned was to stop their reactive incidents by calling for a pause. Realizing they would have to be proactive to master this new skill, they started practicing their pause signal for minor frustrating incidents, such as times when someone felt overloaded or slightly irritated. The first few times they used it, it worked well. But, as we all do in learning a new skill, they occasionally stumbled and fell back into old automatic patterns.

For instance, while cooking dinner together one night, Eric asked Donna, "Should I mash these potatoes more or do you like them lumpier?" Wanting to be helpful, Donna launched into a detailed explanation of how her mother taught her to prepare mashed potatoes: "My mother showed me some things everyone should know. I still find her method the best. I think you'll see why in a minute. The first thing you do after they're cooked is chop the big pieces into tiny pieces with a knife. Then, you add about a quarter of a stick of butter and mash everything together with a fork...." At this point, Eric started getting uncomfortable. He said to himself, "Oh no, she has to give me the whole history here. Why can't she just answer my question?" He recognized a slight tension in his jaw. For a moment, he felt frozen. But because he and Donna had recently been using their pause signal at times like this, he got himself to speak: "Honey, I need a pause."

According to their agreement, Donna was supposed to simply stop talking and not ask for an explanation. Her reactive mind wanted to ask, "Why? Did I say something wrong?" but she was able to simply stop.

Feeling some relaxation in his jaw and in the rest of his body, Eric decided to leave the kitchen — just to get some space for a minute. Before exiting, he glanced at Donna, as if asking for permission to leave, but he couldn't read her facial expression. Feeling a little less relaxed than the moment before, he left the room anyway — intending to come back and finish the potatoes a few minutes later.

Seeing Eric walk away triggered Donna. She was already thinking, "What did I do?" And now she had to deal with another unknown, "Is he coming back? Is he upset with me?" Her survival alarm went off, and all she could feel was a mounting anxiety that seemed to need immediate attention. She bolted out of the kitchen looking for Eric, calling out, "Why did you have to leave so abruptly? That was hurtful and rude! Here you go just thinking about your own needs and ignoring what I need."

She found Eric down the hall in the study, looking at his computer. The first thing she noticed was that he did not look up as she entered the room. This triggered her even further. The pair exchanged a few short accusatory outbursts, and they were at it again — caught in their familiar vicious cycle.

After going around and around, Eric began to feel an over-whelming tiredness. He pleaded with Donna, "I am very ex-hausted. My brain is on overload. Could we please take a break for just a little while?" Donna was running out of steam, too. She agreed to pause, saying, "Okay. I'll give you the space you want, but we need to talk soon about how this marriage is not really working for me anymore." With that parting shot, she left the bedroom and went back to the kitchen to put away the half-prepared meal.

They slept in different rooms that night. In the morning,

both of their nervous systems had calmed down somewhat. Eric entered the kitchen cautiously, trying to read Donna's mood by her body language. She looked stiff, but he took a risk and asked, "Can we hug?" Hearing those reassuring words from her beloved, Donna's body softened. She moved toward Eric to receive his embrace. Letting out a big sigh, she relaxed and felt her defensiveness ease. She said, "I'm sorry I overreacted. I realized later that you were trying to do something good, Eric. You were practicing our pause signal when you interrupted my explanation about the potatoes. Isn't that what you were doing?"

Eric appreciated this acknowledgment. He said, "Yeah. But I forgot to say that I knew we'd work this out and that I only needed a short break. I see that I need a lot more practice interrupting things when I feel overloaded or upset. I don't like to show it when I'm upset. I try to get away from those feelings as soon as possible. But running from my feelings is not working for me anymore. Since we're starting to get more real with each other, it's getting harder to fool myself into thinking I'm always reasonable."

Donna smiled. She loved hearing this. Feeling safer, she also apologized: "I'm so sorry for what I said about this marriage not working for me. I didn't mean that. Not at all. I was triggered. Can I take that back?"

"Okay, honey. I'm willing to let it go if you are. Is there anything I could have done differently in calling for a pause? Is there anything we can learn from this?"

"I think I got triggered when you left the kitchen without saying anything."

"So, it would have been better if I had said I needed to take a break and would return in a few minutes?"

"I think that would help. Would you be able to do that?"

"I will try. I like knowing specifically what to do to make things work better."

"I do, too. I think we are making progress, and that feels good to me, that you are really trying — that *we* are trying together."

"Yeah. We'll probably have to practice this new skill before we really get good at it. I want us to try this pause signal again before the end of the weekend. I think I might be kind of fearful about trying it again — since I didn't do such a good job this time."

"You did great," Donna countered. "I appreciate you so much for being willing to try it. I guess it'll be my turn to initiate it next time. I'll try to remember to say, 'I need a pause,' and leave it at that. Can I trust you to stop right away? No parting shots like I did."

As he heard her words, he thought, "I hope so. I hope I can learn to feel safe here." So he shared, "I really want us to work. This makes me think of something my mother always said, 'If at first you don't succeed, try, try again.' It'll be easier to try new things if I know neither of us is going to quit. I guess I need reassurance that we won't give up."

"I have a similar need for reassurance. I would never leave you. I have to learn to stop threatening you with my words."

"Yeah. Thanks."

This incident reveals one of the pitfalls of trying something new. When people try new behaviors, it usually takes patience and practice to get good at it. During this practice stage, you might not have all the new moves you're going to need to halt or prevent a vicious cycle. So you both need to agree to try and try again.

The other challenge when first using the pause tool is that, after initiating a pause, you might have difficulty calming yourself so you can become resourceful again and get back online with all your IQ points. This, too, takes continued practice.

Pausing Is Crucial, but It's Only the Beginning

As Donna experimented with using their pause signal, she became very frustrated at times. She would think to herself, "I call for a pause, but I still feel upset. What's the point? Calling for a pause doesn't get rid of my anxious feelings."

This is important to remember. Calling for a pause does not make upset feelings disappear. Instead, after pausing, you must use the self-calming tools you will learn in later chapters. But pausing *does* stop you from escalating your reactivity even more. It's Rule No. 1 about finding yourself in the Hole: stop digging!

Pausing is crucial because it gives us the opportunity to calm down. What are the alternatives? If Donna continues reacting, she and Eric will have an even harder time recovering. She knows from experience it is best to stop triggering each other earlier rather than later. The sooner they stop, the less time it takes for them to calm down and get resourceful — and the less damage they have to repair.

Why don't we all realize this? Because the reactive mind is seductive. It will trick us. The Hole says, "Jump in here! There is gold in here this time. If you can just get your partner to hear you, this will get rid of your upset feelings. If your partner would just understand you, everything would be great. Your partner is wrong, and you can prove that you are right. This time your partner will finally realize it!"

As compelling as this inner voice may feel, it offers illusions. Have you ever truly resolved an issue by overpowering your partner? Don't let your reactive mind trick you into thinking you can get rid of your upset if only you can establish that you are right. Of course, after you have both calmed down, it is important to understand each other, but this is the last step in the process. First, notice your reactivity and pause, then stop to calm yourself, then practice the communication tools described later in this book. This is the way to feel really safe and secure with a partner.

A Formal Pause Agreement

If you and your partner agree about the value of pausing, here is a formal contract that you can fill out together and sign. We highly recommend that you download and print this contract from the "Pause Agreement" section of the online workbook (available at www.fiveminuterelationshiprepair.com).

1. Our pause signal is _____ [examples: "I need to pause," or "Time out"].

2. Each person's job is to give our pause signal as soon as he or she detects reactivity or signs that one of us is triggered. It is our job to be alert for signs of distress and then quickly call for a pause.

3. When our pause signal is given, we both will stop talking. We will also cease any and all nonverbal reactive behaviors (such as rolling eyes or slamming doors). When possible, we will also offer each other the kind of reassurances of safety we know we each like (supportive touch, hugging, reassuring words).

4. We will discuss and agree on how long a pause period is needed. The length will be determined by whoever needs the most time to calm down.

5. During our pause period, we each will calm and reassure ourselves that we are safe — that although we may feel upset, there is really no tiger nearby. We will prepare to come back and engage in constructive communication to repair what happened.

6. We will not use a pause to avoid issues. We will return to and repair each rupture caused by our reactivity. We will aim to resolve our issues in a way that is fair and works for both of us.

Signed,

_____

_____

Chapter Three

Calm Your Overactivated Nervous System

CALLING FOR A PAUSE offers a way to stop your survival alarm from taking over when you get triggered. But then what do you do? How exactly do you calm your nervous system to recover your higher brain capacity?

This chapter presents several tools to calm yourself and regain your resourcefulness. Many of these tools have been used for centuries in traditions of self-mastery, such as yoga, martial arts, and meditation. They help train your mind so it does not fall so easily into reactive feelings. With practice, you will develop the ability to stay calm, centered, and resourceful in almost any situation. Try each of the tools to discover which works best for you.

Slowing Your Breath

This tool involves actively changing how you breathe. In it, you deepen your in-breath and slow down the exhale.

> Take in a deep breath through your nose. Breathe all the way down to fill up your belly and all the way up to fill up

your chest. Breathe out very slowly through your mouth. Now time your inhale and exhale. In your mind, count to three for the in-breath, and count to six before you reach a full exhale. Three counts in. Six counts out.

Practice this for a few minutes. Afterward, notice how you feel. Once you get used to this form of breathing, try a more advanced form: inhale for three counts, pause for three counts, and then exhale for six counts. You can also add in a count of three after each exhale before you start the next inhale. Experiment to discover which of these breathing practices works best to create a sense of inner calmness.

Breathing Awareness

For this tool, don't count or try to control your breathing. Just pay attention to how you are already breathing naturally.

1. Notice your chest and how it expands and contracts with each breath. There is nothing to change or get right. For the next minute, notice the speed of your breathing and the depth of each breath.

2. Move your attention to your belly button, and sense the movement there with each breath. Notice the speed and depth of each breath for another minute.

3. Now pick the place you found it easiest to track your breath — in your chest or belly. Notice how the movement of your breath going in and out resembles a wave. The top of the wave is when you finish inhaling; the bottom is when you finish exhaling.

4. Follow this wavelike motion. Notice which part of the wave feels the most relaxing: the top, the bottom, or somewhere in between. Now let your attention

rest more fully into the most relaxing part of the wave for each breath.

Resting Your Attention in Your Belly

The following tool will help you get more skilled at resting your attention in your belly. Go through these steps slowly.

1. Move your attention down into your belly. Notice the rise and fall of your belly as you breathe in and out. Note the speed and the depth of each breath.

2. Now move your attention to the floor of your abdomen — about an inch below your navel, deep in the center of your body. Sense how it rises and falls with each breath. This movement is very subtle.

3. Experience this rise and fall as resembling a gentle wave on a calm lake. Imagine a little boat on that lake. Rest your attention in that little boat. Notice which part of the wave — the rise or the fall — feels the most relaxing.

4. When you notice that your attention has wandered to a thought, just say to yourself, "That's a thought." Choose not to follow it; perhaps say, "I'll get back to that later." Then return to that gentle wave, and rest your attention in the little boat a bit longer.

5. Over the next few minutes, repeat this process. Whenever you notice a thought going through your mind, just say, "That's a thought. I can get back to it later." Then return to the little boat and rest your attention there a while longer. With each breath, notice the slight rise and fall of each gentle wave.

As you practice resting your attention in your belly, you will grow your capacity to sense small changes in your breathing, to come back to your body sensations, and to relax your mind whenever reactive thoughts take over.

When we get triggered, the reactive mind takes over our attention. We worry about what might happen. We fume over what did happen. Such thoughts trigger higher levels of activation. When this happens, move your attention back to your breath. Move away from the thoughts in your head that upset you.

Sensing a Chair Holding You

Here's another tool to help you regulate your own nervous system. If you are not sitting in a chair right now, find a place to sit that feels comfortable and supportive to your body.

1. Notice the chair you are sitting on. Feel all the places the chair makes contact with your body — your pelvis, your back, your legs, your rear end, and everywhere else.

2. Locate the place in your body that feels the most deeply held by the chair. Notice how the chair supports the weight of your body, your bones, your muscles.

3. Relax more deeply into the chair and notice how it feels throughout your body — paying attention to exactly where the chair supports your body.

4. Over the next few minutes, let yourself rest in the chair. If you notice your attention wandering, just say, "That's a thought, and I can get back to it later." Then gently return your awareness to your body being held by the chair. Rest your attention there for a while longer.

Relaxing Body Tension

This powerful tool involves intentionally letting go of all the tension in your body. Do this while sitting down in a comfortable chair.

> Scan your body with your awareness. Notice any sensations of tension or discomfort. It could be tightness in your belly or tension in your jaw. Your shoulders might be raised or your neck feeling a bit tight. Whatever it is, each time you notice something, see if you can let go of the tension and relax that part of your body. Just scan and relax each point of tension as much as possible.
>
> Scan from head to toe and back again. Accept whatever you find, embracing it with your awareness, while intending deeper relaxation.

An advanced form of this tool is to combine body scanning with feeling a chair holding you. Notice how the chair supports your weight and how comforting this feels. Sense how relaxation naturally spreads as you allow your weight to be supported by the chair. Then scan again for areas of tension or discomfort. You may notice that these have become (even slightly) more relaxed. Now move your awareness back to feeling the chair again, resting your attention on how relaxing it is to be held by the chair. When ready, scan again for any areas of discomfort and notice how they may have further changed. Keep going back and forth for a while — moving your attention between being held by the chair, followed by gently scanning your body for tension.

Chapter Four

The Power of Frequent Coregulation

THE PREVIOUS TWO CHAPTERS presented tools to pause and self-calm whenever your survival alarm gets triggered. Using these tools, you can teach your nervous system to self-regulate when you would otherwise escalate to higher levels of activation. This chapter presents a practice you can use to calm your partner and cultivate a deep and abiding sense of safety in your relationship.

The term for this practice is *coregulation*. Coregulation refers to how one person offers reassurance to another in ways that calm the person's nervous system. This is done through key behaviors that speak directly to the person's emotional centers without interference by the logical mind:

- ❖ Touch that is supportive, such as a hand on the shoulder or a comforting hug
- ❖ Eye contact, using a soft, loving gaze
- ❖ Voice tones that are soothing, such as speaking slowly and softly
- ❖ Saying short, reassuring phrases like, "We're okay" or "We'll work this out"

Coregulation is primarily a biological phenomenon that is delivered body to body. Consider how other species soothe one another and calm distressed nervous systems. Cats and dogs lick and huddle their bodies together. Monkeys hold and groom each other. Humans use touch, holding, eye contact, and reassuring voice tones.

Also, think of what soothes a distressed one-year-old child. Children feel secure and safe when they are held, experience eye contact, and hear a soothing voice. They may not understand the words themselves, but these simple nonverbal behaviors send a message of reassuring safety to any human nervous system — including in adults.

Coregulation helps a distressed partner's nervous system calm down. More importantly, consistent nonverbal reassurance will change a person's wiring so that he or she is less likely to get triggered. Eventually, a nervous system that gets frequently coregulated by another person will learn to automatically regulate itself. For a couple, it's as if you are reparenting each other, helping each other heal old emotional wounds caused by parental abuse, neglect, ignorance, or preoccupation.

Coregulation Fosters Self-Regulation

Frequent coregulation by a partner leads to better self-regulation. Each act of coregulation increases the ability of your higher brain to regulate your alarm system, and it aids your ability to correct false alarms. You can use this practice to help calm each other right before you take a pause. Often a little coregulation before a pause will shorten the time needed for the pause. Sometimes, it might even eliminate the need for the pause.

Recognizing when you are triggered, then pausing and engaging in physical coregulation can dramatically increase your sense of safety in a relationship. Think of yourselves as teammates cooperating to manage reactivity. If either of you notices that a member of the team is running toward the Hole instead of the goal line, you call for a time out to pause and stop moving forward. Then you get into a huddle with your teammate, with a hug or some other form of reassuring touch. Once your nervous systems calm down, you're ready to get back to the game.

Secure partners are aware and resourceful enough to notice when one person is triggered and to reach out and hug or lovingly touch that person. The effectiveness of such coregulation depends on many things, including how triggered you were before you paused.

For instance, say a pause is called, but you agree it only needs to be for a minute or two. Before saying anything else, you might ask for a hug and say something reassuring like, "Thanks for pausing. I really like how we can do this together!"

On the other hand, let's say your survival alarms have really taken over and you are both highly triggered. Voices rise, interruptions prevail, and accusations are flying. Finally, one of you calls for a pause and says, "I'll need an hour before I can continue discussing this topic."

You agree to separate for an hour and come back together. It's still helpful to first engage in some physical coregulation. You might say, "Okay, but could we please hug first? I know we can get through this and eventually get back to feeling good." That brief hug and reassurance can help you both calm down a bit before you separate.

A basic foundation for feeling safe in a primary relationship is the availability of physical coregulation. Be liberal with supportive touch and hugging, especially when someone is upset. Learn to take a breath, slow down, and shift your own voice tone so that it is soothing and calming. If you speak, say something friendly. Reassure your partner that he or she is important and/or that everything will be okay. Say "I love you." Mention something you appreciate about your partner. These simple moves can do a lot to calm down alarms that have been unintentionally set off.

Frequent Coregulation Changes Brain Wiring

Beyond its use as a tool to navigate triggered states, coregulation is a powerful practice for helping both partners feel more consistently safe and secure. It helps you hear and respond to each other better, no matter what the subject is — even potentially charged topics.

Frequent coregulation builds a foundation of mutual appreciation, safety, warmth, and well-being. It reassures us that we are safe, that we matter, that we are accepted and valued. It wires in stronger connections between higher brain centers and the alarm system. This leads us to associate being in our partner's presence with feeling safe.

One of the major advantages to being in a primary relationship is the availability of coregulation from someone we depend on. Being comforted when we're in distress adds to our inner sense of strength and resilience when we face life's many challenges. Perhaps this is one of the primary gifts of the fact that biologically we are dyadic creatures — that we are designed to pair up. It pays to take advantage of this gift that nature has given us. The strongest source of coregulation for us as adults is with our intimate partner. It can be remarkably life-enhancing and even life-extending.

Many of us have opted for self-sufficiency as the preferred way of handling difficulties, when nearby we have a partner whom we could lean on. Research shows that frequent coregulation is not only good for emotional well-being. It also dramatically benefits physical health and longevity.

I Want to Hold Your Hand

A study done by Jim Coan and his colleagues demonstrates the power of coregulation.* Women were placed inside a special magnetic resonance imaging (fMRI) machine, the type of device hospitals use for brain scans. While inside this machine, the women were periodically shown one of two letters, an "X" or an "O." If an "O" appeared, nothing at all would happen. But if an "X" came up, then some moments later the women might feel a shock on their ankle. Brain scans of the women during the experiment showed how areas of the brain associated with reacting to threat were quickly activated if an "X" appeared, whether or not a shock followed. Nothing surprising about that.

However, on certain trials, the woman's husband would be present, holding her hand. In cases when the woman's hand was held, the level of activation in the wife's alarm system was considerably reduced. In other words, having her hand held by her husband directly downshifted activation in her survival alarm. These women also reported experiencing less physical discomfort or pain when a shock did occur.

Incidentally, a stranger holding a woman's hand would also reduce her perceived pain, but only by half as much as when her husband held it. Note that this deactivation was accomplished simply by hand-holding. Because the women were inside a large fMRI machine, eye contact and broader supportive touch was not possible.

These results demonstrate the power of coregulation to ease distress. There is nothing more powerful for the nervous system than supportive touch, eye contact, soothing voice tones, and

---

* James A. Coan, Hillary S. Schaefer, and Richard J. Davidson, "Lending a Hand: Social Regulation of the Neural Threat Response," *Psychological Science* 17, no. 12 (December 2006): 1,032–39.

simple reassuring messages. From infancy through adulthood, these are the behaviors that calm us and help us feel safe.

Secure Couples Coregulate Often

Ongoing coregulation is vital for a healthy and secure human relationship. When there is distress, partners who respond to each other with these coregulating behaviors promote secure functioning. But even when there is no distress, securely attached couples coregulate as a normal part of daily life together.

Whenever partners depart or arrive, they connect. Coming home is greeted with hugs, eye contact, and welcoming voice tones. They embrace or kiss before they leave for work, and they hold each other before they go to sleep at night and when they awaken in the morning. Essentially, because they received this kind of coregulation in childhood, they naturally tend to want it, ask for it, and give it freely and frequently.

If you have not experienced much physical coregulation with a partner, the above may sound excessive. Usually, if you feel uncomfortable with such behaviors, it reflects a lack of consistent touch, holding, and eye contact received from your own early caregivers. But you needed these things then, and you still need them now — probably more than ever! Even if you never received much coregulation as a youngster, your nervous system will still respond to coregulatory support today. This is the most fundamental medicine we can get and give each other to heal reactive patterns in relationships.

What Are Your Relationship Habits?

Reflect for a moment on each of these questions regarding how you tend to relate with an intimate partner:

❖ How often do you *engage* in touch or eye contact as a part of daily relating?

❖ How easily do you *ask for* touch, hugs, or eye contact as a *normal* part of relating?

❖ How easily do you *offer* touch, holding, or eye contact when your partner is upset?

❖ How often do you *approach your partner and ask* to be held, touched, or given eye contact when you are upset or stressed?

❖ How do you *respond* to touch or eye contact from your partner?

If your answers to the questions above reflect that touch and eye contact are sparse in your relationship, you might want to change that. A great time to hold each other and gaze into each other's eyes is whenever you and your partner separate or reunite throughout the course of a normal day.

To increase your awareness of what would feel good to you, do the following visualization exercise:

1. First, review in your mind's eye what you do now when you and your partner separate and reunite. Play the movie in your head of a typical scene when someone arrives home. Imagine it as if you are watching two actors on a screen.

2. Now be the director of that movie. Ask the actors to change the emotional tone of the scene so that it looks like your ideal of a loving couple reuniting. Have the actors engage in warm physical touch, hugging, eye contact, and friendly greetings. Watch the scene again, letting these loving elements emerge in their own way.

3. Go through several more takes of the scene, making suggestions as the director, until the actors finally do it just the way you'd like it to be.

4. Now jump into the screen and merge with the actor who is playing your part. Do that scene again, this time experiencing it as the person arriving home or greeting the other's arrival. Notice the gleaming eyes and smiling face of your partner, who is so happy to see you. Sense the warm physical touch and supportive feelings in your embrace.

If you are interested in increasing the frequency of physical coregulation in your partnership, this visualization is a good start. Then talk to your partner about bringing these behaviors into your daily life, so that you engage in more supportive touch and physical warmth with each other.

Start a Hugging Practice

If you both agree that you want to increase the coregulatory behaviors in your relationship, here are a couple of practices you can use.

Consciously engage in hugging with your partner. This may be uncomfortable if you do not normally hug each other — especially if you have unresolved issues. The practice is this: while hugging, feel any sensations in your body that indicate tension or discomfort — and then keep hugging until you feel yourself relax. It may take several minutes to feel sufficiently relaxed. Some couples prefer to do this while lying down together. Do this hugging practice in whatever position feels right to both of you, and feel free to experiment with different positions. Anyone can change position at any time to find more comfort in the connection.

Couples therapist Stan Tatkin takes this practice to another level and suggests that you hug until you feel *your partner's* body relax. As you embrace, close your eyes. Feel the palms of your hands on your partner's back. Don't rub or massage your partner.

Just keep your hands still, and focus on the sensation of touch. See if you can sense your partner's muscle tension and breathing. Notice as your partner's body shifts to a more relaxed state. Stay with the practice until you feel his or her body relax; meanwhile, your partner is doing the same for you. Again, allow yourselves to shift your posture anytime to increase comfort in the connection.

Hugging is not holding still like a statue. It's a process, with the goal being relaxation. Let yourselves be as fussy as you want; shift your body, in any way and at any time, to maximize comfort. Especially notice your head and neck positioning. A shorter partner may crane the neck back, which is not comfortable to sustain. If your neck cranes back, try repositioning your head to curve slightly down, tucking your face into the soft cushion of your partner's chest.

Doing these practices whenever either of you arrives home will establish new, positive experiences of coregulation in your life together. If you make this a priority over anything else that needs to be done, it will create a stronger bond between you. If you have kids or pets, they will also benefit from your greater relaxation and calm.

Asking for a Hug, Eye Contact, or Supportive Touch

Many of us still need to develop the skill of requesting supportive touch. By asking for what you need, even if it's new, you give your relationship an opportunity to heal you.

If asking for touch feels new or risky, either to you or your partner, then it can help to make an agreement together to add more coregulation to your life. This can be as simple as agreeing that both of you can ask for supportive touch at any time, and that the other will always agree to respond positively. Or, you could be more formal and specific. Here are some possible elements of such an agreement.

❖ We agree that it's good to ask to be supportively held, hugged, or touched.

❖ We agree that it's good to ask for eye contact.

❖ We agree that it's good to admit when we feel distressed and want supportive coregulation.

❖ When asked, we will respond positively, with some appropriate form of coregulation.

❖ We will give and receive coregulating touch predominantly in silence.

❖ When we are coregulating physically, we will track our body sensations and stay in contact until we relax (and until we feel each other relax).

❖ While in contact, we can shift body posture to increase physical comfort. Being fussy is encouraged. Being stiff or uncomfortable will block coregulation.

Use this agreement to intentionally bring more coregulation into your interactions. Aim to be generous and responsive to your partner's requests. Certainly, there may be times when you won't want to be that close — even if it could help. Sometimes you may be too activated. Don't force it. This agreement is not meant to trap you or to become obligatory. Be especially mindful if one of you has a fear of being trapped or controlled. Coregulation is meant to soothe activation, not to trigger it further. If one of you has significant difficulty with methods of coregulation like hugging for several minutes or maintaining eye contact, find an alternative. For instance, if frontal hugging is triggering, try side-to-side body contact or even back-to-back. If steady eye contact is too uncomfortable, use brief but frequent intervals of eye contact.

Don't wait to ask for coregulation until you feel distressed. Ask for it when things are calm as well. Introduce it as a practice to increase your overall sense of connection.

While you are receiving supportive touch, practice asking

your partner for the specific kind of touch you want, whether it be a hug or the placement of a hand on a particular part of your body. When receiving, let in your partner's support. Experience how it enters your nervous system. Move your attention out of your head and into your body. Track all the sensations associated with the touch your partner is offering. It's usually best to do this primarily in silence. But feel free to report your sensations and feelings if you wish.

Giving Supportive Touch

It's important also to find out what kind of supportive touch your partner wants. If you are new to this, you might experiment with some of the options listed below.

- ❖ Put your hand on your partner's shoulder or fore-arm.
- ❖ Put your palm on your partner's heart.
- ❖ Put your hand on your partner's back, behind where he or she feels sensations of distress.
- ❖ Put your hand on your partner's front where he or she feels sensations of distress.
- ❖ Hug in a standing position.
- ❖ Sit together on the couch and hold your partner.
- ❖ Sit with your partner's head on your lap as he or she lies on the couch.

Experiment and combine techniques. For instance, sit together comfortably on a couch and place your palm on or near where sensations of distress are located in your partner's body. Or sit on the couch, allowing your partner to lie down with his or her head in your lap, and rest your palm on top of the heart area. The best kind of touch for coregulation is steady, solid, still contact using your palm, rather than massaging, patting, or moving your hand. Your palm is a superb energy-sensing device. Tune in to whatever you can sense with your palm as it touches your partner — breathing, muscle tension, energy vibrations. Simply being calm, steady, and attentive will coregulate your partner.

Though coregulating touch is best done in silence, if you both agree, describe or discuss what you are both sensing, so you can adjust and improve the experience. Ask your partner about his or her body sensations and if they change with your touch. Are relaxing or nourishing sensations showing up? Occasionally ask if your partner would like a lighter or firmer touch or to change the location or position of your hand. As your partner feels relief or relaxation, maintain this position for a while to stabilize this experience.

You can also notice and share your body sensations. This will keep your attention focused on the present instead of on your fear stories. Whatever is said, be an empathetic listener. In essence, you want to communicate, "You are all right. We are safe. We will get through this together." Coregulation promotes self-regulation.

Frequent Coregulation Helps Lessen False Alarms

Sometimes, when your safety alarm gets triggered, danger *does* lurk nearby (though it's rarely a tiger anymore). Still, the fact is that most of the time you experience a false alarm. You don't need to rapidly get more energy into your limbs or anesthetize yourself. As you get good at self-regulation, you will be able to self-correct false alarms and avoid going into states of fight, flight, or freeze.

Frequent coregulation with your partner strengthens the braking mechanism in your brain, improving self-regulation. Instead of having an accelerator stuck to the floor — going full speed to the Hole — your nervous system can slow down and give you breathing room to make different choices.

Partners with good self-regulatory circuits can move more slowly through conversations about issues or potentially charged topics. There are natural pauses in their discussions — plenty of room for both parties to be heard and understood. They feel safe together, even as they discuss something that could otherwise trigger reactivity.

For trust and intimacy to flourish, we all need to get better at detecting false alarms. And we need to quickly catch and put a halt to reactivity when alarms start to ring.

Recall the first story about Donna and Eric in chapter 1. Donna was triggered by Eric's flat voice tone as he gave her advice about her boss. If she had been better at self-regulation, her higher brain might have been able to reassure her that she was in no real danger and that Eric's response did not indicate a lack of love or respect. After her initial trigger, she would have realized that Eric had no ill intent and that she was safe with him.

With better access to her higher brain, she would have asked for a brief pause, giving her time to discharge her anxiety and discover what had triggered her. She might have told Eric, "I appreciate you for wanting to help me solve this problem — and I want to hear more. But right now, I'd prefer if you just held me. Then I'd like you to just listen to my feelings about what happened at work. It feels so good being held in your arms and having you hear me."

But as it does with most of us, Donna's survival alarm took over. Instead of receiving an automatic self-reassurance of safety, the meaning-making part of her brain tried to explain her escalating levels of adrenaline with a story: "Eric is talking down to me like I'm stupid! He doesn't respect me!" Believing this worst-case analysis, she spoke out defensively and angrily, which triggered

Eric. This trigger-upon-trigger situation is extremely common. The term for this is *cotriggering*.

Receiving coregulation improves brain wiring. It helps us develop a stronger connection between the part of the brain that gets activated and the part of the brain that can spot false alarms and reassure us of safety. If, as children, we were held when we were distressed, then we developed a better capacity to self-regulate. If we did not get held enough in childhood, then we need to receive more coregulation now.

Couples who realize this will do their best to put the brakes on any distressing interaction and provide coregulation as soon as possible. They hold each other in some way until a sense of calm returns. And they do it even when they are least inclined — when they feel upset or triggered. This paves the way for repair, constructive discussion, and problem solving.

Cotriggering Is Inevitable, Coregulating Is a Choice

When a partner's alarm is ringing, it is almost impossible not to get triggered as well. Below the level of your conscious mind, neural circuits continuously detect the emotional state of other people, as reflected in nonverbal cues like facial expressions and voice tones. You may or may not be consciously aware of these cues. But your subcortical brain is always scanning like radar, and your alarm may quickly become activated if your partner's face or voice appears to be that of a foe rather than a friend. Also, through what scientists call *limbic resonance*, your partner's state of distress may be duplicated within your own body without anyone realizing it.

The bottom line is that if your partner is triggered, you will soon feel triggered, too — and vice-versa. On the other hand, if you consciously act to stay relaxed and open, your partner is more likely to return to a calm state, especially if you engage in coregulation.

So whenever anyone's survival alarm is activated, cotriggering will naturally occur — unless we do something to change it. It is at this point that we reach an important intersection: one road escalates the conflict and leads to the Hole, and the other road goes in the opposite direction, in which we coregulate, downshift activation levels, and reassure each other that we are safe.

Most reactive incidents are under way before you realize it. Usually, by the time you do recognize you are activated, you have already unconsciously cotriggered your partner. Only when we become more aware of triggering — even at low levels — can we change this automatic pattern. Once you recognize the signs of activation, you can pause and calm yourself, then use physical coregulation to reassure each other. When coregulation is needed, words often confuse things more. Words are too often used as a cover-up for feelings. Instead, through physical touch, you put each other solidly on a new road to overcoming reactive cycles.

Chapter Five

Your Brain Makes Up Stories
That Trigger You

About nine years into their marriage Eric and Donna were hoping to get some of the passion back by making a date night part of their weekly routine. At that point, they had not yet fully recognized how their sense of intimate connection was being eroded by so many years of unrepaired upsets.

One particular date night led to a significant triggering event. Despite having an important work deadline Eric would have otherwise stayed at the office to meet, he went on the date anyway, since he did not want to risk Donna's disappointment by canceling. However, during the meal, he occasionally glanced at his cell phone to see if his partners, who were working late that night on this critical project, were trying to reach him.

Donna had been eagerly anticipating an evening of Eric's undivided attention. She had really been looking forward to this evening together. But Eric's frequent lapses in attention eventually got to her.

After noticing Eric looking at his phone for the fourth time, a familiar story arose in her mind: "Even on our date night, his work is more important than I am. I'm always second priority." She began to feel a familiar knot in her stomach.

Her frustration continued to build as they ordered their meal. When the server left the table, she complained sharply to Eric, "At least the waiter listens to me!" This sent a shock wave through Eric's body. There was a familiar sense of danger and a sinking feeling in his chest. A familiar story came up in his mind: "I can never satisfy Donna. Nothing I do is ever enough for her. I planned this fabulous date night, and she's still not pleased. She can't see how hard I'm working to provide for us — even now, trying to close this huge deal. You can't win with this woman!"

On the surface, Eric tried to seem calm. He ignored Donna's comment and changed the subject to their kids, thinking that was a relatively safe topic. He didn't want their evening to be ruined by some seemingly unnecessary conflict. But he didn't stop checking his cell phone. Donna's frustration grew. As her adrenaline level increased, and her stomach churned, her storytelling brain took over: "I'm all alone here at this table — and in this marriage. Eric is just not interested in me anymore. He never asks about my life or my needs."

After finishing their meal, they ordered dessert. Typically, they would share a dessert when they went out, so when Eric ordered the cheesecake, a dessert that Donna didn't like, she finally erupted: "You're always so self-centered! You know I don't like cheesecake! All you care about is what's important to you." Her eyes were glaring and her nostrils flaring.

At this, Eric's inner alarm started blasting. A sinking feeling extended all the way from his throat to his belly. A familiar story played in his head: "This is hopeless. I can never please her. She expects me to read her mind!" Feeling numb and blank, he grew silent. He didn't know what to say.

Eric and Donna finished their meal in uncomfortable silence.

Driving home, Donna was fuming. Eric was stuck in a frozen state. They ended up sleeping in separate rooms.

As outside observers, we might be astonished that Donna and Eric couldn't simply express their needs more directly to each other. We may wonder why they had not long ago discussed and resolved issues around interruptions from work and how something so small could provoke such big reactions.

But they did not yet understand how one's survival alarm system can quickly hijack the higher brain's capacity to engage in rational problem solving. Years of unrepaired upsets had led each of their primitive brains to expect the worst, thus producing their mutually feared outcomes.

Compounding this was the fact that romantic coregulatory behaviors like eye contact and physical touch had diminished over time in their relationship.

In the next chapter we'll discuss the dynamics of reactive cycles and how our brains are programmed in childhood to fall into predictable patterns of reactivity. And over the next few chapters, we will see how Donna and Eric developed a deeper understanding of their triggers as well as the emotional language to repair triggering incidents.

The Mind Creates Stories

When your brain's alarm system is triggered, it initiates a state of fight-flight-freeze in your body. Once your higher brain receives these danger signals, your mind tries to make sense of why your body is in this state. Not realizing how brain chemistry works, most people believe and act according to whatever stories their minds come up with. Under stress, the part of the brain that makes meaning of what is going on seems to formulate worst-case stories. Instead of reassuring us that we are safe — that there is no cause for alarm — this part of the human brain fabricates quite a different story.

In this book, we call this our *storytelling brain*. It is the part of our wiring that concocts meaning. This meaning-making function is generally considered to be located in the brain's left hemisphere. The explanations provided by our storytelling brain usually justify why our alarms are ringing: "My feelings don't matter." "I'm never appreciated." "I always come last." "Nothing I do is ever enough." This kind of self-talk escalates activation, and we become even more upset.

Such stories can become an internal source of self-triggering that persists long after an incident is over. Eventually, these explanations coagulate into more rigid and long-lasting stereotypes that limit how we see each other and our relationship. This shifts how we feel about each other and sets up negative expectations that become self-fulfilling prophecies. For instance, Eric starts to "see" Donna as someone who is always upset, so he starts defending himself as soon as she opens her mouth to speak. Donna starts to see Eric as someone who is always resistant to her requests, so her voice becomes anxious and strident whenever she asks for his attention. When we believe the stories our minds make up, we make our fears come true.

These mistaken assessments can keep us in a state of constant vigilance, always on the verge of being triggered. As they continue over time, they take us ever deeper into the Hole, where seeing and hearing what's actually happening becomes impossible. So it is of critical importance to recognize how the stories in our heads originate and how damaging they can be.

It pays to remember the wise adage "Don't believe everything you think!"

When Eric heard Donna's reaction at the restaurant, he had no idea what she was really feeling. Of course, her communication did not help him understand this, either. So his storytelling brain manufactured an explanation: "Donna doesn't respect me. She is never satisfied. Nothing I do is ever enough!"

As his activation level escalated, Eric's mind built a case to justify this story: "Here you are, Eric, taking her out to a special restaurant — after working so bloody hard all day long! Even now you're still trying to make sure that big deal at work succeeds. Does Donna ever appreciate what you do for her? Does she even respect you? No! She has no idea how much hangs on this deal. She thinks money grows on trees. There's nothing you can ever do that will satisfy this woman! It's just hopeless! Why do you even bother?"

Meanwhile, Donna had her own inner story: "I always come last, after his work. I'm not sure I matter at all to Eric. Here we are on our date night, and I'm all alone!" These stories triggered even higher levels of activation. For the moment, they thought these stories were true.

The Story Is a Self-Triggering Event

Just like Donna and Eric, when we believe whatever our storytelling brain fabricates, we are pushing our own buttons! As we listen to this sort of mind chatter, our survival alarm quickly escalates to higher levels of activation. Then our upset reactions seem completely justified!

Even after the reactive incident, we can keep escalating our own upset as our brain replays these stories again and again. With time and repeated unresolved upsets, people become even more convinced that their stories are true. Partners begin to see each other through the filter of mistaken generalizations.

As their stories take over, partners lose the ability to understand each other accurately. Did Donna have any idea that Eric was also hoping for a romantic night of reconnection on their date? Did Eric have any idea that, for Donna, going on a date meant having his undivided attention? They each mistakenly believed the other did not value them, did not care about their feelings, or did not want to connect.

You probably hear such worst-case stories in your head when you get triggered. Next time this happens, notice your self-talk. Is there a common theme — like how insensitive your partner is, or how you always come last? Can you see how believing such stories gets you even more upset?

The meaning-making part of your brain seeks to establish cause-and-effect links between things. In many situations, this helps you function well. It's good to have a predictive model for how things work and how to stay safe in the physical world. You learn to look both ways before crossing the street, predict how billiard balls will rebound, and think four moves ahead in chess. So the analytic brain is quite useful for many things in the world, especially where simple rules apply.

However, for matters as complex as human relationships, the analytic ability of your brain is often not quite up to the task, especially when your primitive alarm starts to ring. That voice in your head that explains what is going on can easily get it wrong. You know this well, since you have probably been misunderstood by others many times. You at least know that other people's brains get it wrong. But you've got one of those storytelling brains, too! And not only is it severely limited when it comes to understanding relationships, it may be causing a lot of damage to your love life. When the storytelling brain processes information, it will over-simplify, and it will arbitrarily connect the dots based on past experience and past unfinished business — not on present reality!

Stories Are about "Why"

In the 1940s, before effective pharmaceutical drugs were discovered, brain surgeons found they could cure severe epilepsy with an operation that separated the left and right sides of the brain.

In this radical surgical procedure, doctors severed the corpus callosum, a major channel of connection between the brain's right and left hemispheres. This prevented the interhemispheric thunderstorm that causes seizures, and thus saved patients' lives. As a result, though, most information no longer flowed between the two halves of the brain.

Neuroscientist Michael Gazzaniga realized that these patients provided a rare opportunity to look at how each side of the brain functioned in relative isolation.* In the 1960s, he started over four decades of research on patients who had had this operation. In one study, he projected a silly picture that was only visible to the right visual field of a patient, who would then start laughing. Then he asked the patient, "Why are you laughing?"

The patient did not know, but the storytelling brain (in the brain's left hemisphere) would still fabricate an answer. The patient would say something like, "This is a funny projection machine," or "You guys are running a silly experiment here."

In another study, Gazzaniga projected a frightening movie that was only seen by the patient's right brain. The patient reported feeling nervous. Asked why, the patient quickly claimed that Gazzaniga's research assistant looked a bit creepy. Even though the patient's upset feelings were triggered internally in the right brain, the left brain asserted that the cause was a random person in the room.

Through years of such inventive studies, Gazzaniga conclusively demonstrated how the meaning-making part of the brain ad-libs and just makes things up. It makes up stories that sound like reasonable explanations for what we are doing and feeling, or what the other person's behavior means. And we believe these stories as if they were facts.

---

* Michael S. Gazzaniga, "Two Brains: My Life in Science," in *Inside Psychology,* ed. Patrick Rabbitt (New York: Oxford University Press, 2009), 101–16.

In a similar way, when our alarm gets triggered, and we do not realize what is truly setting it off (which we will discuss in the next few chapters), our brain makes up a story: "My partner doesn't care about my feelings," or "I can never please her." It is as if a frightening movie starts playing in our right brain while we talk with our intimate partner. We start feeling and even acting upset, but we don't recognize the cause. When our partner asks, "Why are you so upset?" we blurt out our story: "Because you never listen to me!" or "Because you always have to be right!"

Stories That Keep Us Triggered

What stories come up in your head when you get upset? The following list shows some of the more common stories that come up when there is distress in our love lives. Check off any stories that your mind has fabricated when you were triggered by a partner. Change the pronouns "he" and "she" to suit your situation.

This exercise is in the online workbook's "Reactive Stories" section (available at www.fiveminuterelationshiprepair.com). You will refer back to this list later in chapter 8.

- ❑ "I am all alone."
- ❑ "He shuts me out."
- ❑ "She is so distant."
- ❑ "I am way down on the list."
- ❑ "I always come last."
- ❑ "He just doesn't seem to care."
- ❑ "My feelings don't matter."
- ❑ "We are never close anymore."
- ❑ "She is not that into me."
- ❑ "I am just not sure I matter."
- ❑ "It's like he doesn't see me."
- ❑ "I don't know how to reach her."

❏ "If I didn't push, we'd never be close."
❏ "He doesn't really need me at all."
❏ "Nothing I do is ever enough."
❏ "She doesn't appreciate me."
❏ "I can never get it right, so I give up."
❏ "I must be flawed somehow."
❏ "I feel like a failure as a mate."
❏ "It just all seems so hopeless."
❏ "I try to keep everything calm."
❏ "I try not to rock the boat."
❏ "I go into my shell where it's safe."
❏ "I am just not as needy."
❏ "She just gets overemotional."
❏ "I can handle things on my own."
❏ "I don't know what he is talking about. We're fine."
❏ "I try to fix things, to solve the problem."

Why Are Our Stories Worst-Case Scenarios?

We formed our basic beliefs and expectations about relationships with our first significant others — our parents and early caregivers. How we were treated by them, and how we saw them treat one another, led to the expectations and interpretations our minds continue to feed us today. This programming continued with siblings, friends, peers at school, and any other meaningful relationships where we sought to get our needs met.

If we experienced emotionally painful or frustrating events, this installed certain fear buttons in our brains. Here are some of the common fear buttons that show up in intimate partnerships. These include the fear of being...

abandoned, rejected, left, all alone, unneeded, insignificant, invisible, ignored, unimportant, flawed, blamed, not good enough, inadequate, a failure, unlovable, controlled, trapped, overwhelmed, suffocated, out of control, helpless, weak.

Which of these have you ever felt in a significant love relationship? Such fears can get triggered by any event that seems similar to a past incident where our significant needs were frustrated.

Donna's fear button of being not good enough was connected to the way her father used to lecture her about how she should act in school, how she needed to perform better in some class, or how she could improve herself. As a child, Donna got the message that she was not lovable. A core need for being accepted and valued seemed to be threatened when her father launched into his lecturing tone. Hearing Eric use a similar voice tone triggered this fear button, and the story came up in her mind that "Eric is talking down to me like I'm stupid!"

Donna had not yet learned that her storytelling brain was leading her astray. In the same way, Eric's inner storyteller misunderstood Donna. He grew up with parents who argued constantly. He felt helpless and scared when he heard their loud voices, and he usually ran and hid in his room. So as an adult, he would easily fall prey to the story that he was powerless when someone got angry or raised their voice around him.

Donna and Eric are like the patients in the experiment, where they had no real idea why they felt afraid or upset. But their minds filled in the blanks with stories. So if you find yourself getting upset, it may serve you and your relationship to pause and question any story about "why" that comes into your mind.

When you're upset, get in the habit of asking yourself:

"What if I'm inaccurate in how I see this?"

"What if my story is simply what I *fear* to be true?"

Chapter Six

Secure versus Insecure Relating: From Infancy to Adulthood

MOST OF US REALIZE THAT INSECURITIES, fear buttons, negative expectations, and sensitivities were programmed into us by past experiences. We understand that once a fear button has been installed, we become vigilant, cautious, or self-protective from that time forward. At the root of this is an alarm system deep in the brain programmed to scan for signs that past neglect, abuse, or frustration is happening again. Operating in concert is the storytelling part of the brain, which systematically feeds us worst-case generalizations ("If I open my heart, I'll get hurt") and interpretations ("He doesn't care how I feel"; "Nothing I do is ever enough") that mirror our childhood programming.

These fears get automatically projected onto our partners, affecting how we view events, what we expect to happen, and how we react. Unconsciously generated, this projection takes place without our permission. The process operates like all conditioned reactions: we know that being bitten by a particular dog in the past can program a phobic response to any dog in the future.

Generally, the younger we are when a disturbing event

happens, the more unconscious power it will have. Events that occurred in infancy, when our nervous systems were least resilient, have the most power of all. These triggers can also be the least obvious to us — especially if the original pain occurred before we had words.

Before two years of age, our right brains are dominant. Most of our information about our safety and security comes via our caregivers' vocal tones, touch, facial expressions, and gestures — through nonverbal communication. We learn whether crying brings us relief or punishment. Maybe we come to the conclusion that we need to scream to be heard. Or perhaps we find that it works better to clam up. Whatever we learned then is probably reflected in how we express ourselves today.

Our patterns of emotional expression as adults are largely shaped by how we were treated before age two — and by how we witnessed family members treating one another. Some lucky children felt loved, accepted, and respected and saw their parents relate to each other in healthy, loving ways. As adults, these are the people who seem to instinctively know what to say and do to develop healthy partnerships. They have a rich emotional vocabulary and a wide behavioral repertoire, thus giving them the resources required to respond creatively rather than automatically to life events.

But most of us did not receive optimal caregiving. We didn't learn the communication skills to successfully resolve issues with a partner or repair the emotional rifts that occur when alarms start ringing.

Optimal caregiving means receiving fairly consistent coregulation, such as receiving regular supportive holding, touch, eye contact, and reassuring voice tones. This fosters healthy development of the neural wiring involved in detecting false alarms and feeling safe with a significant other. If we did not get optimal caregiving, then the development of our neural wiring got short-changed, and we will experience more insecurity as adults.

Research over the last couple of decades has uncovered the key factors in how childhood conditioning affects our entire lives. These new revelations offer important insights and tools to help us unlearn faulty conditioning, reprogram our nervous systems, and meet needs that were not met in childhood. It's not too late to learn the skills needed for healthy, secure relating. Through mutual coregulation, we can build more resilient and responsive neural pathways in our brains and expand our current repertoire, giving us the ability to build healthy loving relationships.

This chapter explains how we get trained in childhood to communicate emotional needs, and it describes what you can do now to fill in the missing pieces in your past emotional learning.

Coregulation in the First Two Years

Much of communication is a matter of signals and responses. We send out a signal ("I need a hug") and hopefully get the response we seek ("Let me hold you"). When we signaled our needs as infants, such as by crying, our caregivers ideally offered supportive touch, friendly eye contact, and soothing vocal tones. These responses are the body-to-body biological messages that let our nervous systems know we are safe. This signal-and-response process starts at birth; we come out crying and, hopefully, are quickly placed on our mother's breast to receive skin-to-skin contact. This birth imprint would have told us, "Welcome to a safe world, little one." These actions bring regulation to an upset nervous system. Ideally, our caregivers continued to coregulate us during childhood whenever we were distressed or in need.

If we do not get the response we need, we will change our signal. In some cases, our distress signals get louder — cries turn to screams, fits, and tantrums, and we may find it much harder to settle down when a parent finally does respond. In other cases, we may give up and stop signaling our distress. We shut down our feelings. We learn these communication patterns even before we learn to use words. The quality of our cry — whether it gets amped up, shut down, or remains innocent and vulnerable — is programmed by the quality and consistency of the responses we get from the adults around us.

In your first two years of development — before your left brain started developing its complex verbal language capacity — physical coregulation from a caregiver let you know you were safe. As any responsive parent can attest, nothing works better to calm a distressed infant than supportive touch, holding, eye contact, and a reassuring voice tone.

Did your parents hold you when you cried? As you became more active, did you run to them when you were hurt or upset? How did they respond? Their responses impacted the early development of your brain circuitry and how you learned to express yourself emotionally.

If children get coregulated fairly consistently, they learn how to communicate emotionally in a way that maintains a sense of security. As adults, they will automatically transfer this into words and actions that create love and happiness in their relationships. Studies show that the more consistently infants are given relief for their distress in ways that include coregulation, the more able they are to feel trusting and secure in their adult relationships.

Coregulation in infancy is a biological process that promotes vital connections in the developing brain. These neural connections provide the higher brain with the means to self-regulate the survival alarm and to keep false alarms from taking over. Partners with well-developed higher brain circuitry are able to stay in tune with each other and quickly repair upsets.

Optimal Caregiving for Emotional Security

When we are around six months old — as we start to crawl and explore the world — the ideal parents support us to explore while helping us feel safe and secure. Their consistent coregulation sends the message: "I'll be here for you when you feel fear or upset. If you feel a need to connect, just signal. I am here to give you loving attention and respond to your needs. I will hold you and help keep you safe from danger. Otherwise, I'll give you plenty of room to explore. You can trust that I've always got your back."

In this optimal situation, if some unfamiliar event or object frightens us in childhood and we cry, our parents will hold us. If we go to them, they will look into our eyes reassuringly. If we explore new territory, we can look back and see them watching us and feel safe to keep going. This teaches us to realistically assess danger. Their responsiveness also teaches us that our feelings and needs matter to other people.

In this way, an infant learns: "I am safe to show my distress or my needs. I will receive quality attention from my caregiver. My feelings are valued."

How We Learned to Communicate

Take a moment and imagine hearing your adult partner tell you, "It's safe to show me your needs and let me know if you feel upset or distressed in any way. I am here for you. I care how you feel. If you're unhappy, I won't overreact or try to talk you out of it. I want to really listen to you. I want to hold you and reassure you that you are loved and safe."

How would this affect how you communicate with your partner?

Now imagine yourself saying these same things to your partner. This will be a lot easier to imagine if you experienced healthy bonding and coregulation when you were little.

Experiences with early caregivers provided our initial training in how to trust relationships and how to express our feelings. Typically, we did not receive a reassuring response every time we were vulnerable and distressed. Depending on the amount of missing or negative responses we received, we may have learned to expect that others would not be interested in our feelings.

That's what happened to Eric. As a child, his parents rarely picked him up when he cried. They believed this would spoil him and make him too dependent, and so Eric learned to shut down his crying. Meanwhile, Donna learned she had to scream to get attention, instead of expressing feelings in a vulnerable, direct way. Both Donna and Eric learned to act out their feelings through reactive behaviors. So as adults, their capacities to express feelings were still underdeveloped, and they easily fell prey to states of fight, flight, or freeze.

Luckily, anyone can heal these sorts of reactive tendencies, no matter what happened in childhood. And there is no better person to do this with than your significant other. It's never too late to have a happy childhood! We can give each other now what we missed then.

For a moment, imagine that Donna experienced different childhood programming. What if she had received more consistent attention and responsiveness from her parents? Then as an adult, she would be able to express her feelings more vulnerably. Instead of reacting with anger when Eric gave her advice, she would notice her inner resistance and realize that, instead of advice, she needed him to listen. She would be able to say, "Eric, I appreciate your help, but right now, I'd really appreciate it if you could just listen to me talk about it. Would you do that?"

Or, if she started to get annoyed by Eric, she would catch her reactivity before it escalated, since her nervous system would have developed the resources to do so in childhood. She might interrupt her reactivity and ask for support: "Could we just pause for a moment? And can I have a hug?"

If Eric's emotional resilience had been more developed in childhood, he could catch his reactivity when Donna voiced her complaints. He would be better able to calm himself, hear her, and express his real needs.

Secure Functioning in Intimate Partnerships

Securely functioning partners trust that their distress matters to each other and will be responded to in a positive way. Secure partners believe, "It's safe to tell you when I feel distressed or have a need. I am not afraid to show emotional vulnerability." They have a sense that "I can depend on you. I'm not worried you are going to leave. And you can depend on me. So I can ask you for help easily, and you can ask me for help easily."

Secure partners believe that if there's a rift or rupture in their connection, it will get repaired. They think, "No big deal. We'll reassure each other that we're safe, resolve the issue, and keep moving forward together." They don't automatically assume that a relationship is threatened if there is disagreement. They trust their ability to perceive accurately and communicate effectively. Though they may experience differences, they can listen openly to each other and be empathetic. Their alarms don't hijack their higher brains or their abilities to communicate.

Secure partners place a high value on respect for differences. Decisions have to make sense and be good for both partners. Secure partners will tend to be collaborative rather than competitive.

With secure functioning, there is an ease of flow between being together and being alone. Secure partners can interrupt their solitude and easily make a friendly connection when the other person wants to make contact. On the other hand, they don't get triggered or feel abandoned when that person does something independently.

Have you ever wanted to connect just when your partner needed alone time? This is a common source of distress in relationships. It can lead to triggering and reactivity. But if we are functioning securely, it's relatively easy to shift between connecting and separating, between contact and being alone. If your partner is busy, you can wait to connect later. Or if you are busy, and your partner wants contact, you can easily shift and connect — even if just for a minute.

How Securely Functioning Partners Communicate

Securely functioning partners feel safe to reveal vulnerable needs and feelings. They can talk about anything, knowing that if conflicts or misunderstandings occur, they have the tools to resolve them. If they feel distressed or have a need, they'll express it at the appropriate volume level. They won't have to turn their volume way up in order to get attention. It won't be mixed with angry protest or anxiety. They won't shut their signaling down or hide out. They will admit their needs and their fears and reach out for reassurance. And if either partner notices that the other is distressed, they will quickly respond with touch, eye contact, and simple, soft, reassuring messages. Each partner knows what their partner needs to feel safe, and they know how to calm and reassure their partner when needed.

Coregulation is a natural part of a secure couple's daily life — not only in response to distress calls, but as a way to nurture their sense of connection. Secure couples touch often. Partners may frequently hug at departures and arrivals and check with each other throughout the day. Even when they are apart, they will still feel connected.

Secure couples know that interdependence is the root of healthy, happy relating. They know that, as couples therapist Stan Tatkin says, "Relationship is like a three-legged race." Ongoing happiness is based on both partners staying vertical and moving forward together. The basic rule is: "If you fall, then I fall." You cannot leave one partner on the ground.

Taking a stance that treats their relationship as a three-legged race, secure partners know that it is in their *own* best interest to find mutual solutions — and to respond in a caring, helpful way when a partner is in distress. A secure couple has no interest in who is right or who will win if there's a difference in needs. Partners work together to arrive at a solution that works for both.

As in a three-legged race, if one person feels off balance, that person needs to know how to reach out for help in an open, transparent way as soon as possible. If a distressed partner needs reassurance, the other knows how to quickly respond with co-regulation or comforting verbal messages. Secure couples get triggered, but they have learned how to accept their triggers and quickly reassure safety or repair.

How Securely Functioning Couples Handle Distress

All couples go in and out of synch and will occasionally be at odds. Distress occurs even in the best relationships. How such distress is handled makes all the difference.

The following steps summarize what a secure couple will do if someone is distressed or gets triggered. This sequence is described from the point of view of *you* being the partner who gets triggered. Of course, it could be the other way around.

1. You notice that you are upset, distressed, or triggered.
2. You approach your partner and express your distress in a simple, vulnerable way.

3. Your partner responds by coming forward to coregulate and reassure you.

4. This calms you and helps you feel safe again.

5. It also helps you trust that your relationship can handle occasional upsets.

6. Your connection is strengthened, and your overall trust is deepened.

In a secure partnership, if you get distressed or triggered (either by your partner or by some life event), you know it is your job to approach your partner for reassurance. You do not expect your partner to read your mind. You don't avoid your feelings or keep them hidden. You do not try to provoke a response through baiting or indirect requests. You do not blame or guilt-trip your partner. If you catch yourself in a reactive pattern, you notice it and revise your approach as soon as possible.

When triggered, secure partners will give a simple, direct distress signal (such as, "Ouch," or, "I just got triggered"). Just like a secure child, they will readily show their need for reassurance. Secure partners will reveal their soft, vulnerable feelings, core fears, and core needs to each other.

On their date night, if Donna had felt secure (as Eric was checking his cell phone), she might have said: "Eric, you've been working so much lately. I'm starting to miss you. I'm feeling lonely. I need to feel our connection more. I'd like to hold hands while we're sitting here…and maybe later lie on the sofa and cuddle."

In this example, Donna readily admits her core feelings and asks for coregulation. Approached this way, Eric would have felt safe. He might have responded with empathy and reassurance, expressing through touch, eye contact, a soft voice tone, and words, "You are safe with me. We are together. Our love is strong."

Even if Eric could not give Donna exactly what she wanted,

if he were operating as a secure partner, he could listen and offer empathy. He could appreciate her willingness to ask. This type of coregulating response promotes self-regulation in each other.

Secure Couples Quickly Calm Each Other's Distress

We would all prefer to feel and act more like a securely attached couple. We learn to function more securely as we develop the capacity to express our needs simply and vulnerably, to reach out for hugs and reassurance, and to respond to our partner's distress.

An easy way to foster secure functioning in your partnership is to become proactive in offering reassurance. As soon as you notice your partner is triggered or in distress, don't wait to be told. Offer coregulation and reassurances of safety right away.

Be an early responder. Remember, the longer you wait, the louder survival alarms will ring. And if your partner's alarm is ringing, yours will soon be ringing, too. It is best to calm distressed states as soon as possible. The longer a couple stays in distress, the more cotriggering occurs.

Occasionally saying "I love you so much" or "You're the best thing that ever happened to me" can help tremendously. A firm but gentle touch on the arm can quiet inner demons. If you are both triggered — invite your partner to pause with you. Then reassure each other as quickly as possible that everything is okay. Turn your relationship into the safe harbor you may not have experienced as a child.

Do you know what is usually at the core of your partner's distress? You will find this out in the next two chapters. Knowing your partner's core fears provides vital information about what to say to dispel these fears.

As a simple example, let's say your partner was raised to believe that being loved and accepted was dependent on how well he or she performed in school or sports. And you know that your partner feels insecure about being adequate or loved — harboring a deep-seated fear that his or her value depends on being smart, perfect, right, or accomplished. If he or she comes home one day feeling distressed about a poor performance review at work, you know what to say to bolster self-confidence and turn off your partner's alarm. Saying "I think you're great just as you are" can be both reassuring and healing.

Of course, it's easier to offer reassurance when your partner is triggered by someone other than yourself. But even if your own behavior triggers your partner, you can still reassure safety. When you are cotriggered, after calling for a pause, say something like, "I love you. I know we'll get through this."

Your inner sense of safety will grow as you learn how to coregulate each other's nervous systems — in the particular ways that work for each person.

When We Don't Get Enough Coregulation in Childhood

To discover the best ways to calm and reassure your partner, it helps to understand what happened when your partner was a child. If children don't receive enough coregulation and reassurances of safety, their nervous systems will become especially sensitive to certain types of perceived threats. As adults, they will end up exhibiting some form of *insecure functioning*, such as a tendency to hear criticism in a harmless comment.

Research on attachment, or how humans learn to pair-bond, has discovered two modes of insecure functioning — *avoidant* and *preoccupied*. These insecure modes are normal adaptations; they are not pathological conditions. They represent a child's natural adaptation to a type of family culture, where otherwise loving parents simply don't provide enough coregulation — usually because they, themselves, did not get it growing up.

To navigate the rough times in a relationship, we all need

to understand how childhood programming informs our ability to feel secure as adults. As you read these descriptions, keep in mind that there are no pure types. Sometimes our behavior seems "avoidant," while at other times, we may act more "preoccupied."

Growing Up in an Avoidant Culture

Some families do not provide much warm and fuzzy contact such as holding, rocking, and hugging. Such homes are underexpressive when it comes to feelings. In these families, a child will adapt by learning to "take care of himself" — numbing feelings, shutting down self-expression, and keeping busy or distracted.

Parents may be physically present in the house, but when the child is crying or in distress, they rarely respond with comforting touch and reassurances of safety. Children who do not get these kinds of coregulating responses discover they are on their own when it comes to emotional distress. Their nervous systems adapt by finding substitute means to manage distress, such as focusing on toys or spacing out in some way. These children may appear quite self-sufficient. Parents can even leave the room, and the child will hardly notice.

In the past, so-called experts were fooled into believing such a child was confident and autonomous. They routinely advised mothers to resist their urge to pick up their crying infant because this would spoil the child and foster dependency. "Let the kid cry it out," these experts advised. "That way, your child will learn to be more independent." While decades of experts were fooled into thinking the child benefited from this kind of treatment, scientific research now shows this advice to be a perfect formula for creating the type of insecure functioning called *avoidant attachment*. As researchers developed the means to measure stress hormones, they found the avoidant child actually suffers the highest levels of internal distress. These experts on child-rearing got it entirely wrong!

Eric's mom followed the recommended practice of these misguided experts, starting in the first months of his life. As predicted, little Eric did end up crying far less than most kids. He stopped crying and became a well-behaved, self-entertaining boy — much to the pride and joy of both parents. But deep inside, his nervous system was numbing out his distress. His cortisol (stress hormone) levels were extremely high.

Children with this pattern develop a low expectation for getting a calming response from the adults around them. So they stop sending out distress signals and go mute. They stop seeking closeness. They distance, disengage, and withdraw when they get distressed. Sadly, due to unwitting emotional neglect on the part of their caregivers, these children don't see other humans as a source of relief or comfort when they feel upset.

As infants, we are wired to give a distress signal and get a reassuring response. If we don't get such a response — or even worse, if our caregivers leave the room when we cry — we may conclude there is something fundamentally wrong with us for showing our needs. Avoidant children learn to suppress their feelings. They may first learn to trance out on their toys, and then later they do so in their work, their intellectual interests, their hobbies, or their sports activities.

These children weren't displaying the confident independence the child-rearing experts thought they were seeing; they were numbing their anxiety and pain. More recently, researchers observing avoidant children have found that the quality of play they engage in is more dreamlike and less lively than how secure children play. The stress hormone cortisol measured in their saliva is found at a higher level than in any other children. Their nervous systems are trying to self-manage their distress through a trance-like state.

Avoidant as Adults

The avoidant mode is often rewarded in our society, which values speed, efficiency, and performance over our emotional connections with others. Avoidant adults do seem more achievement-oriented. They place a high value on self-reliance. They think they like to be alone, that they are independent. But this so-called independence is not based on a sense of security. They don't like to feel needy, and they don't like to experience neediness in others. They may even fear being swallowed up if they get too close.

Avoidant partners may try to limit intimate contact. They may even feel relief when a partner leaves them alone. Avoidant partners can find it easier to shift from being together to being alone, finding it easier to say good-bye, than to shift from being alone to reconnecting.

Combined with this, avoidant partners also can have a big focus on work or activities. They overrely on nonrelational activities to calm and comfort themselves. It can jolt their nervous systems, like a mini-shock, to suddenly be approached and interrupted by someone while they are working, and they may become annoyed.

Avoidant partners may carry fears of failure or not being adequate. They may worry that a partner will find them not good enough. This emphasis on performance often stems from a childhood in which they received positive attention primarily for their successes.

They will tend to carefully calculate and edit things in their mind in order to avoid upsetting a partner. They worry that if the other person knew what they were thinking, they might lose the relationship. They will be quick to claim nothing is wrong.

This inclination to claim things are fine is an example of how avoidant adults tend to underexpress themselves emotionally. They do not talk much about how they feel, and they have trouble responding when a partner expresses emotions. They will tend to stay in their head, rationalize, intellectualize, give advice, defend themselves, or in some other way push feelings away. This is all because they never were shown by a significant other that their emotional states matter and that their feelings can be discussed. They simply have not yet learned that talking about feelings can lead to relief of distress.

Instead they may tend to get overwhelmed by emotional content and want to escape. They can seem allergic to discussing past events: "The past is the past. Why do we have to keep going over it? What good is it? Just let it go and move on."

Giving advice is their typical response to a partner's distress — offering intellectual help, using reason to fix things or explain things. They do not recognize the coregulatory power of just listening or offering physical coregulation.

When they get triggered, they will usually start ignoring, acting reasonable, withdrawing, or shutting down, like Eric did when Donna got upset about his cell phone on their date night. This can make it seem like people who operate in the avoidant mode don't care about others or don't have feelings. On the contrary, avoidant partners are suppressing their feelings in order to deal with the extreme distress of their own self-doubts and insecurities. Shutting down occurs because they are so sensitive, and their nervous systems are so easily overwhelmed. Thus, they need to keep things calm. Withdrawing is preferred because they believe that expressing their feelings will only make a situation worse.

Growing Up in a Preoccupied Culture

Some families tend to make warm physical contact and hugs available quite a bit, although inconsistently, or parents may be overexpressive when it comes to emotions. Trying to get a coregulatory response from a parent may even come with a cost, like "Stop being such a cry-baby," or "I'll give you something to cry about!" In such a home, the child sometimes gets held and sometimes not, depending on the feeling state of their caregiver. The preoccupied mode of insecure functioning results when parents are responsive some of the time but inconsistently. It may seem to the child that getting positive attention is random, like flipping a coin.

Sometimes the parent is right there, hugging, kissing, eye gazing, and responding with affection. But at other times, instead of being attuned to the child, the parent is "checked out." Many factors can produce inconsistent responsiveness in a caregiver. He or she may be consumed or overwhelmed by his or her own emotions and unable to respond to the child. The child's distress may push the parent's buttons. Or the parent's unmet emotional needs might spill out onto the child. When this occurs, the child is forced into a painful role reversal, where the child attempts to regulate the parent's state.

Regardless of how it happens, the uncertainty of getting a response leads to a background state of anxiety or anger in the child. The child's alarm system becomes highly sensitized, monitoring the caregiver's every move. The child's radar is up. These children always seem to question, "Are you going to be there for me this time?" Anger can build up for all the times the parent did not respond. So when the parent finally does show up, these children do not readily calm down. They may harbor some form of angry protest or be flooded with anxiety. Not receiving a consistent coregulatory response at this critical developmental period, the child's brain does not develop stable self-regulation circuitry.

Donna's mother tended to have emotional highs and lows. Her mood swings interfered with her ability to consistently respond to her child's cries. Sometimes Donna's mom did hold her and rock her. But just as often, her mom was absorbed in her own emotions and did not do this. Worse yet were the times her mother's upsets spilled out onto Donna. As a result of this inconsistency, little Donna showed signs of being anxious and angry by the time she was one year old. She adapted to her family conditions with a form of insecure functioning called *preoccupied attachment*. (Researchers also use terms like *ambivalent, anxious,* or *angry-resistant attachment* to refer to this insecure mode.)

The preoccupied mode of functioning looks like what our society would call clingy or needy. Children in this mode seem to suffer stronger abandonment fears when the parent leaves or gets focused on something or someone else. When preoccupied children are distressed, they signal it louder and longer. Angry protest will often be mixed into their signals. Even before they have language, the child seems to be asking, "Are you really there for me? Do you love me? Can I ever really be secure with you?" When the parent does respond, the child's anxiety is difficult to soothe. Doubt lingers: "Even as you hold me now, can I really trust you to stay?" While being held, preoccupied children may squirm, hit, kick, cry, or yell. It's as if their nervous systems have to dramatically amplify their distress signals to get attention because of a lingering doubt they will ever be adequately and consistently soothed.

Preoccupied as Adults

Adults in the preoccupied mode tend to feel anxious about whether a partner is really there. They strive to feel connected, and they pursue closeness. In daily life, preoccupied partners find it harder to say good-bye and separate; they find it easier to shift from being alone to reconnecting. They are sensitive to withdrawal. They tend to harbor fears of being alone or abandoned.

Partners in the preoccupied mode tend to talk a lot. It often takes them a long time to say anything. Too much silence makes them anxious. Talking calms them down and makes them feel better. They can be very expressive and easily jump from one topic to another — not noticing when this overwhelms their partner. They like to say everything, to think out loud. Meanwhile, the listener may tend to check out due to information (or emotional) overload.

Preoccupied partners may doubt their self-worth, believe they are overbearing, or that they are a burden. They look for signs they are not important and worry that their partner doesn't care about the relationship as much as they do. If they think they are not being heard, their distress signals may get louder and longer.

When Donna and Eric were on their date night, Donna was triggered as Eric checked his cell phone, and she fell into a preoccupied mode. The stories she fabricated revealed core fears of abandonment: "I am not as important to him as his work. Our date night is not as special for him as it is for me. I'm all alone."

Preoccupied adults will feel like they have to keep knocking on the door to get in to really connect with a partner. But their form of knocking will be some reactive behavior like prodding, questioning, or complaining. They worry that if they don't pursue, they will never get a response. This may soon escalate to criticizing, attacking, or blaming — typical reactive behaviors of a preoccupied pursuer.

Some preoccupied partners have a tough time being comforted. They may at times seem to push a partner away with angry protest: "I don't trust you. I'm not going to relax. You're going to abandon me all over again." Although they seek closeness, they expect or fear the worst — further abandonment. When this results in reactive behaviors like complaining or criticizing, the person's partner is usually triggered to withdraw — which activates even more fears of abandonment.

In contrast to the avoidant adult, who just wants to move forward as quickly as possible and forget the past, a preoccupied partner has a tendency to bring up the past and rehash old disappointments in an attempt to regain a sense of connection.

Insecure Functioning in Your Relationship

Partners operating in the preoccupied or avoidant mode tend to behave in ways that bring about the outcomes they fear most. Instead of seeking or offering reassurances of safety, they react aggressively, defensively, or self-protectively. This, in turn, triggers resistance or resentment. Over time, partners spiral down into deeper levels of distress. After a while, almost anything they discuss winds up triggering both of them. They cannot just speak from their hearts, openly, simply, vulnerably, and undefended. Instead, they communicate using a metaphorical *sword* or *shield* — depending on which insecure mode dominates their nervous system.

Everyone has access to both sword- and shield-like behaviors and will use one or the other depending on the circumstances. Likewise, any of us can behave as more avoidant or more preoccupied, depending on many factors. In general, the more one partner becomes a preoccupied pursuer, the more the other will behave like an avoidant withdrawer — and vice versa.

Let's look in detail at how communicating with a sword or shield perpetuates a couple's sense of danger.

Communicating with a Sword

When Donna starts acting like a preoccupied pursuer, she hides her softer core feelings and needs behind a sword — complaining, criticizing, prodding, questioning, provoking, pressuring, making suggestions, yelling, or blowing up.

Deep inside her soft heart, Donna is trying to say things like: "I miss you. I want to connect. I'm afraid I don't matter to you. My old fear of abandonment is getting triggered." Essentially, she needs reassurance that she is important to Eric. She wants to feel connected. If she felt safer, she'd probably say something like, "Will you please hold me and reassure me that I matter to you so I can feel connected with you?"

But because of the preoccupied culture she experienced in her family, the emotional language patterns her brain developed didn't include the vocabulary of a vulnerable, direct request. As an adult, she still doesn't realize vulnerability is an option — so she reaches for a sword instead, imagining this to be the more powerful alternative. This echoes how she used to erupt in angry protest, scream, or get clingy in childhood.

Donna may think she is only knocking on Eric's door, asking to be let in to receive emotional connection from him. However, clanging on his door with a heavy metallic sword sends out a different sort of message. Eric takes her critical words and harsh voice tone as a rejection, as evidence that she does not value or accept him. In response, he can either get out his own sword or put up a shield. Having grown up in an avoidant household, Eric favors the shield as his main defensive tool, and an all-too-familiar pattern of escalating reactivity is set in motion.

Communication with the sword is fueled by reactive feelings like anger and frustration. Donna makes accusations: "You don't care. You're cold and insensitive. You only think about yourself.

You always…You never…" Donna has no idea that her sword-like communications scare Eric.

Communicating with a Shield

Eric has learned to disengage or defend himself in an effort to calm things down. He pulls out his shield, using logic, reason, or distracting conversation.

Deep inside his soft heart, Eric may be trying to express things like: "I'm afraid you don't accept me. I fear I'm not good enough. My fear of rejection is getting triggered." He, too, would like to reach out for reassurance that he is accepted and valued by Donna. If he felt safe, he'd be able to ask, "Will you please hold me and reassure me that you accept and value me as I am, that you don't require me to change in order to be acceptable?"

But Eric was seldom comforted or reassured in childhood when he felt upset. He learned to just go to his room and deal with his feelings on his own, mainly by numbing out and trying to distract himself with toys or stories of adventure he would make up in his head. His nervous system never learned it was possible to directly express his distress to another human being or that his feelings would even matter to someone else.

When Eric does things like walking away, pushing feelings away, lecturing, and staying in his head, he thinks he is only trying to keep things calm. But to Donna, he appears to be closing the door to her, shutting himself off in another room. This type of behavior will often trigger a partner's fear of abandonment.

Eric has no idea Donna's alarm system interprets his distancing behavior to mean, "You don't matter. I don't like being close to you." That is how communication with a shield is often interpreted by others — who will either put up a shield themselves or use a sword in an attempt to break through and connect.

However, no matter what we experienced in childhood, and

no matter what type of insecure functioning we exhibit, it's never too late to develop a deep sense of emotional security. The nervous system can self-modify. We can all learn to feel safe and secure — even if we have never felt this with a partner. We can learn to communicate in ways that get our real needs met — our needs to know and be known, to love and feel loved.

In the next few chapters, you will learn more about how reactive cycles work so you can transform reactive patterns and use upsets to strengthen your love and sense of security.

Chapter Seven

Take Stock of How You Communicate

MOST OF US SUFFER FROM SOME DEGREE of insecure functioning without realizing it. Our personalities are riddled with defensive habits that block our capacity to speak openly about our
feelings and needs. This developed in infancy, as a result of the
caregiving we received, and it differs for each of us, depending on
our specific circumstances (see chapter 6).

It is part of the human condition to have insecurities buried
deep in the unconscious mind. These insecurities will, of course,
live on into adulthood and affect how we express our feelings and
needs in relationships. But it really is possible to heal our patterns
of insecure functioning — and to help each other heal in the context of a secure adult relationship.

The first step in self-healing is developing the ability to objectively observe how you show up in life — how your personality
has constructed itself to help you feel safe in the world. The way
to do this is by being curious about your patterns of verbal and
nonverbal communication — those patterns that make it difficult

for you to hear a partner's upset feelings or to express your own feelings and needs.

If we could recall what it was like when we reached out for connection or reassurance at the age of six months, we would have an easier time understanding how our communication patterns began. Most experts hold, however, that our ability to remember only goes back to around age two. So in many cases, our insecurities originated before we had the words to describe our experiences.

To gain more awareness of our automatic patterns, it is useful to look in some detail at what we *can* remember from childhood and identify events that were painful, frustrating, or uncomfortable. Most of us — even if we have not had therapy — can remember some events in childhood that may have led to sensitivities, insecurities, or reactive communication habits.

Here is one of Eric's early memories of how he was treated: "I am in my bed crying in a darkish room. I must have been about three years old. I am upset that my mother isn't home. She was a working mom and sometimes didn't get home until late. I am pounding on my bed and crying. My grandma comes in, tells me to stop being a baby and to act like a 'big boy,' and then leaves. So right away I stop crying. I feel sad and resigned. I shut down."

For avoidant children like Eric, the only way his brain found to calm itself was by disengaging, numbing the pain of not having his needs met, and adopting some substitute strategy — like staying busy with toys, being compliant, being good, and trying to be invisible.

One of Donna's childhood memories was going with her mother to a medical appointment: "She tells me to stay in the waiting room while she goes into the doctor's examination room. I am four. I am afraid to be left alone. I tell my mom I want to go in with her. She ignores me and walks away, disappearing into the next room. I get up to follow her. She comes back and pushes me down into a small child-size chair and tells me to shut up. I start screaming that I don't want her to leave me. She keeps walking away. That's all I remember. I think I was shaking and crying — because I was so scared and because I thought she didn't care about me. I wonder if that incident had anything to do with why I was always so afraid when my mom would leave me alone. Maybe I thought she was trying to get rid of me."

Preoccupied children like Donna may suffer a pattern of fearing abandonment and then acting clingy. When these children do not get what they want, they can react by yelling, throwing tantrums, or by engaging in some form of angry protest. As adults they may feel so much anxiety around their needs that they come across as manipulative or bossy.

How We Learn the Wrong Thing

Unfortunately, the emotional vocabularies of both Eric and Donna were shaped by their early frustrating experiences trying to get their needs met. Thus, they learned to reach for a sword or shield instead of expressing their needs in an open, vulnerable way.

This is an example of learning the wrong thing about how to get your needs met. Many of us had similar frustrations growing up, whether we remember specific events or not. Maybe we expressed ourselves spontaneously and were hurt or frightened by an adult's reaction of anger or criticism. Or we were so often ignored that we drew the conclusion that "It does no good to express my needs. No one will respond."

Few of us are encouraged to fully express our feelings as children. So most people end up with negative expectations around expressing needs. When these get triggered, we rely on self-protective strategies we learned in childhood — strategies like pretending not to care or coaxing to get our way.

In this book, we use the term *control patterns* to refer to such unconscious, automatic strategies, which in general are attempts to feel in control rather than to feel vulnerable. Control patterns represent all the automatic ways we have learned to avoid experiencing emotional discomfort — especially the discomfort or pain associated with having our emotional needs frustrated.

Communicating with a sword or a shield are two classic control patterns. There are many other patterns, too. Most of us do not realize how often we speak in self-protective ways. So we get shocked when a partner misunderstands the intent of our actions or fails to meet our needs. If you want to be understood, it's important to become aware of your control patterns and learn to express directly what you feel and need.

Let's start by looking at how your early experiences may have shaped your communication style. This will help you identify which control patterns you resort to when you feel anxious or upset. Once you become conscious of these patterns, you can pause and notice what you are really feeling or wanting and express this instead.

A Self-Guided Tour of Childhood

Control patterns are unconscious communication and listening habits that are so deeply wired into our brains that they have become part of what we think of as our personalities. You can uncover your control patterns by looking at how well your needs were met in early life. To help you do this, take the following self-guided tour of childhood. This describes the needs that all children have growing up — male and female, rich and poor. Slowly read through the list, notice if anything brings up a memory from your own early years, and jot down the thoughts, feelings, and memories that come up.

If you are reading this book with a partner, do the exercise together. Read it out loud and interview each other, taking notes on the memories and feelings that are evoked. This will help you better understand each other's buttons and insecurities.

All Children Need Protection

Did your parents stand up for you? If you felt unprotected, you may have learned to be vigilant about whether you are safe or about who to trust. You might worry about being let down, betrayed, abandoned, or having your boundaries violated. You may be sensitive to not being seen or to your voice not having any effect.

Sometimes this results in the control pattern of giving up or giving in too soon when there is a disagreement. You assume you won't be heard, so why even try? On the other hand, some people develop patterns like being aggressive, controlling, or testing a partner's loyalty. They fear that if they let their guard down, they will be taken advantage of. They look for any evidence they are not being cared for, protected, or respected. They may tend to provoke or even bait a partner when they feel insecure.

All Children Need Loving Attention

Do you have memories of your parents looking into your eyes and expressing appreciation in some way, like, "I love you," or "You're such a great kid." Did they say that for no reason, or only if you did well in school or sports? Did they spend time hanging out with you? Was their affection easily available or inconsistent?

If you did not get such attention, you might have a control pattern of looking for evidence that you are not loved, valued, or accepted the way you are. You may believe your worth depends on how much you do and how well you perform. You may fear being a failure or not being good enough. Or you might be sensitive to feeling neglected, ignored, or abandoned.

All Children Need Coregulation

Do you have specific memories of running to a parent when you were upset or frightened? How did that parent respond? Do you remember getting held, touched supportively, and being reassured in a soft, loving tone? How consistently did each parent offer this when you were upset, crying, or just in need of some attention?

Was there one parent you didn't or wouldn't run to? Did you ever end up feeling you had to handle your feelings on your own? If you lack specific memories of such things, or if you do not remember being touched or held, this suggests that you probably received little coregulation when you were distressed. Today, as an adult, you will probably have a control pattern of hiding your vulnerable core needs behind a sword or a shield.

All Children Need Help Expressing Their Feelings

Can you recall a parent regularly asking how you felt? Did you receive help putting your feelings into words? Parents help us develop an emotional vocabulary by asking us questions like, "How are you feeling? Are you feeling a little sad today because Tommy is away? Do you miss playing with him?" They also help us see what is under our reactions: "Are you mad at Joey? Did it hurt when he called you a sissy?" This helps the child feel okay to be vulnerable and to talk about feelings.

As children, many of us receive little or no help identifying or expressing feelings, so we end up with limited emotional vocabularies. We may especially avoid showing our softer, more vulnerable feelings.

All Children Need Help Understanding Others

Similar to helping children express their own feelings, well-functioning parents help children understand the feelings of others. They ask questions that help children put themselves in the shoes of another person, perhaps to understand the impact we have on others. "Why did Sue call you selfish yesterday? Did she get mad when you took your doll back? Do you think maybe that hurt her feelings?" Questions like these help us understand and accept the emotions of others.

Do you recall having such discussions with your parents? Did they help you see what was going on with your siblings or friends? If you did not learn how to put yourself in someone else's shoes, you may tend to overlook other peoples' needs and feelings. You may get defensive if someone is unhappy with you. You may get puzzled when others see you as self-centered or insensitive.

All Children Need Guidance and Encouragement

Do you recall going to a parent to help you do your homework or learn a new skill (like throwing a ball)? Did they patiently help and encourage you? Do you recall a parent saying anything like, "You have a special talent for science," or "You don't have to be the best. You can make mistakes, and I'll still be proud of you for trying."

Or were you generally left on your own to discover your unique abilities or to learn basic life skills? This can be frustrating, and it can lead to a control pattern of trying to remain invisible. You may have a fear of failure or a fear of being exposed. You may get triggered when someone expects too much of you. On the other hand, you may have become quite independent — not expecting anything from anybody, perhaps thinking nobody can do it as well as you can. In this case, acting self-sufficient and not asking for help would be your control patterns.

All Children Need Helpful Feedback

Many parents expect too much, and the feedback they give is unrealistic and often harsh. Children end up feeling they're not performing well enough. Later in life this can lead to a control pattern of perfectionism or of defensiveness in the face of critical feedback — even constructive advice. Unrealistically high parental expectations can produce a core fear of not being good enough.

Other parents don't give much attention or feedback at all. Their children don't get much information about the effectiveness of their efforts or about the fact that they do have an impact on others. In this case, you might have a button about being neglected or about someone not being there for you.

Taking Inventory of Your Control Patterns

After finishing your self-guided tour of childhood, you may have identified several areas where your basic needs were not met. You may begin to see how your fear buttons and control patterns originated. Ultimately, as children, no one gets all their needs met, everyone develops fear buttons, and we all avoid or cover up our button reactions with control patterns. This is nothing to be ashamed of. It's really important to be able to name your control patterns and fear buttons and accept them as part of the human condition. When we name things that have been largely unconscious, those things have less power over us.

This section helps name some of the most common control patterns. Each item in the list below describes a behavior. Identifying the behaviors that you exhibit will help you notice when you are using a control pattern. Then you can choose your response rather than reacting automatically. You can step back and say to yourself, "I'm doing it again," or "I'm in a pattern here."

Once you recognize a control pattern, you are better able to look beneath this behavior for your authentic feelings and needs.

In the list of behaviors below, check off any you recognize in yourself. You can also do this as a way to identify control patterns you see in your partner (or former partners). If you feel particularly courageous, ask your partner which of these behaviors he or she observes in you. An unconscious pattern may be invisible to you, but it can impact your partner and limit trust and intimacy. Most people find a dozen or more behaviors on this list that they recognize in themselves. Use this knowledge to identify how you may be unintentionally triggering reactivity or mistrust in your partner.

Find this exercise in the online workbook's "Control Patterns" section (available at www.fiveminuterelationshiprepair.com).

❑ Replying too quickly rather than taking in what was said

❑ Obsessing over what you did wrong or might have done wrong

❑ Obsessing about a decision you need to make

❑ Before taking action, reviewing over and over what could go wrong

❑ Taking action or jumping into a situation impulsively, without assessing consequences

❑ Giving gifts or favors in order to win approval or acceptance

❑ Anticipating a partner's needs as a way to avoid some imagined negative consequence

❑ Trying to "help" or "improve" a situation or person instead of expressing your feelings

❑ Making sacrifices for others, secretly hoping they'll do the same for you

- ❏ Asking indirectly for what you want, as in, "Wouldn't *you* like to go out for dinner?"
- ❏ Putting on an act in order to look good or maintain a positive image
- ❏ Blaming your mood or emotional state on your partner
- ❏ Justifying, overexplaining, or defending yourself when someone gets upset with you
- ❏ Reframing things as "for the best" to avoid painful feelings (either your own or another's)
- ❏ Retreating into a world of your imagination, fantasizing about "something better"
- ❏ Lying or withholding information to keep the peace
- ❏ Thinking "this is not a big deal" (to minimize or ignore an important issue)
- ❏ Staying silent or saying, "I'm fine," or "Nothing's wrong," when you are displeased
- ❏ Walking on eggshells to avoid upsetting a partner
- ❏ When someone brings up a past upset, pushing to move forward and "let go" of the past
- ❏ Agreeing too quickly before checking in with yourself about your own needs
- ❏ Telling people what they want to hear while suppressing your needs or opinions
- ❏ Making a joke or cute remark in order to laugh off and avoid your deeper feelings
- ❏ Assuming you hear criticism from others when someone does not mean to be critical
- ❏ Suspecting hidden agendas and double messages, or doubting what you hear
- ❏ Jumping to conclusions about what someone means

❑ Framing a problem or issue in the most pessimistic or negative way

❑ Giving more information or talking more than is asked for or needed

❑ Filling up silences with irrelevant chatter

❑ Overgeneralizing as a conversational habit, talking in platitudes

❑ Instead of staying focused on one issue, elaborating a whole list of issues

❑ Giving advice or making helpful suggestions instead of just listening

❑ Taking a long time to say things, being "thorough," covering all contingencies

❑ Bringing up the past and going over the same topic repeatedly

❑ Repeating what you've already said (when this is not needed)

❑ Telling others what they should do (instead of feeling how their actions affect you)

❑ Obsessing about how things should be or how the other person should be

❑ Lecturing or preaching with a superior tone

❑ Habitually correcting the other person, arguing the point, debating the facts

❑ Labeling, name-calling, or judging the other person (instead of feeling your upset)

❑ Acting angry, forceful, or indignant to get the upper hand

❑ Taking an "it's my way or the highway" stance

❑ Using self-deprecating preambles, such as, "I'm no expert, but…"

- ❑ Questioning like an interrogator, demanding explanations
- ❑ Asking a question and then answering it yourself before the other has a chance
- ❑ Getting sullen or sulking, muttering to yourself
- ❑ Snickering or laughing to oneself in a judgmental or superior way
- ❑ Rationalizing, intellectualizing, or using logic to avoid emotions
- ❑ Protecting yourself from intrusions or demands by avoiding the other person

As you may have noticed, all the behaviors in this list are motivated by a wish to avoid experiencing uncomfortable or insecure feelings. They all hide what you are really feeling or wanting — from yourself and from others. The fact that we frequently use such control patterns indicates how often we do not feel safe enough to reveal our needs, wants, and deeper emotions. These patterns emerged in childhood, when we learned that expressing ourselves vulnerably did not work or just left us feeling even more alone.

Now, as adults, we find ourselves in relationships that in some ways reflect our early experiences in life. But now, armed with greater self-awareness, we can help each other heal from such unfortunate programming. We can become interested and curious about what our control patterns are and what they are designed to protect us from. We can be alert to when we use these to cover up a sense of vulnerability or the fact that we are triggered.

Identifying our control patterns gives us new personal power and new options for relating more intimately and safely. We can learn what our real needs are underneath our attempts to feel in control. We can discover how letting ourselves feel our frustrations, fears, or pains can help us know our true needs and take appropriate action.

Chapter Eight

What's Ringing Your Alarm?

WE HAVE SEEN HOW EARLY EXPERIENCES can lead to secure or insecure functioning. If childhood needs are mostly met, our brains develop strong wiring to prevent false alarms from taking over. But to the extent that our basic needs are frustrated early on, our wiring will not be as well developed. As adults, our higher brains may be more easily taken over when our alarms react. We are more apt to believe the scary stories our brains make up. And we will be plagued by triggers and reactivity in our relationships.

In this book, we refer to any interaction that triggers reactive feelings as a *reactive incident*. Some are obvious, like when one person erupts in anger. Others are not as obvious at first glance, like when you feel disappointed about something but do not tell your partner. Many reactive incidents get brushed under the carpet, only to resurface later in some out-of-proportion way.

Any of the control patterns listed in chapter 7 can cause partners to feel disconnected or out of synch and start a reactive incident. But reactivity can also get stirred accidentally by seemingly innocuous behaviors. As with Donna and Eric, a shift in vocal tone may trigger someone's alarm. Even something as seemingly innocuous as looking at one's cell phone too often can do it. Often an initial triggering stimulus is not clearly recognized and a reactive incident starts before anyone notices. By then, typically, both partners are cotriggering each other.

Here are a few important things to remember about reactive incidents:

❖ If you get triggered, this triggers your partner. A couple's two alarm systems are so highly interactive that they almost always automatically set each other off. For instance, as you get upset, changes in your facial expression and tone of voice start to sound dangerous to your partner's alarm.

❖ When you are triggered, you are under the influence of the strong biological chemicals and the body states of your fight-flight-freeze survival response.

❖ When you are triggered, you automatically fall into one of your reactive behaviors. Rather than communicating about core (vulnerable) feelings or needs, you will tend to escalate your upset or shut down in some way.

This chapter describes the softer, core emotions and needs underneath your reactive behavior and communication. It explains what is really going on when you get triggered and what you actually need to feel safe and secure with your partner.

In a step-by-step process, you will analyze a past reactive incident. With the help of a new vocabulary, you will be able to understand and then speak about what is authentically going on in your heart. This will open new neural pathways, strengthen your brain's wiring, and enable you to stay present and conscious when you get triggered.

Elements of a Reactive Incident

You can look at any reactive incident in terms of what you or someone else did, what you were thinking after it happened, and what you were feeling. A reactive incident usually starts with a triggering stimulus, which can be any verbal or nonverbal cue. Sometimes the triggering stimulus will be words that resemble the criticism of a parent or a parent's lecturing voice tone or upset facial expression.

This triggering stimulus gives rise to thoughts or *reactive stories* — the words that play in your head, such as, "Nothing is ever enough for her," or "He doesn't care about my feelings." After any upsetting event, your storytelling brain will try to make sense of it, filtering it through the lens of past disappointments and fears.

Being triggered also leads to some form of *reactive behavior,* such as blowing up, shutting down, complaining, offering advice, or any of the control patterns listed in chapter 7. You tend to react with habitual coping strategies that help you avoid your real feelings. Remember, not all reactive behaviors are obvious. When you shut down and clam up, this, too, is a reactive behavior.

Accompanying reactive stories and behaviors are *reactive feelings.* The most noticeable reactive feelings are anger, resentment, contempt, disappointment, anxiety, overwhelm, confusion, fear, and going numb. These emotional states will be accompanied by body sensations.

Other types of feelings may be harder to notice. Underneath reactive feelings lies a deeper layer of softer, more vulnerable feelings. These are often overlooked. Later in the chapter we'll discuss these less-visible *core feelings.* For now, let's examine the reactive feelings that get triggered, since these are what foster frustrating or unproductive communication.

As an example, we'll dissect how Donna and Eric thought,

acted, and felt on their ill-fated date night (described in chapter 5). Initially, Donna was triggered when Eric kept looking at his cell phone for messages from colleagues. Initial triggering stimuli can be subtle, even subliminal. In this case, Eric breaking eye contact and checking his cell phone triggered Donna's reaction.

Each time Eric pulled out his cell phone, Donna felt twinges of frustration. She felt a knot growing in her belly. But what really took over her attention were the reactive stories in her head. These escalated her reactive feelings and led to reactive behaviors, such as her complaint, "At least the waiter listens to me!"

Here is a summary of the typical reactive stories, feelings, and behaviors that arise when someone like Donna gets triggered and starts communicating with a sword:

Reactive Stories: "I'm alone." "I'm shut out." "He doesn't care." "My feelings don't matter." "I come last." "I'm not sure I matter." "I can't seem to reach him."

Reactive Feelings: irritated, frustrated, annoyed, angry, resentful, infuriated, enraged, anxious

Reactive Behaviors: pursue, prod, provoke, pressure, question, complain, criticize, yell, blow up

In reaction to Donna's complaining, Eric was gripped by a familiar sense of hopelessness. His chest felt heavy, and the reactive story came up in his head that his efforts were never good enough for Donna. He tried to ignore Donna's anger and talk about other things, but this did not work. Donna's reactive stories persisted, and she became even more agitated and upset. By the end of the evening, their cotriggering behavior, which neither was able to stop, developed into a full-blown fight.

The following summary of reactive stories, feelings, and

behaviors are typical of a partner like Eric who, when triggered, starts communicating with a shield:

Reactive Stories: "I can never get it right." "It all seems hopeless." "I'm a failure as a mate." "I must be flawed." "I need to keep things calm." "I'm trying to solve the problem."

Reactive Feelings: hopeless, stuck, blank, empty, numb, not feeling, confused, paralyzed, ashamed

Reactive Behaviors: withdraw, ignore, hide out, avoid, distance, space out, shut down, stay logical

As we've seen, Donna and Eric's reactive behaviors cotrigger each other. We refer to this circular pattern as a *reactive cycle*. The more Donna pursues and criticizes, the more Eric ignores and withdraws, and vice versa. In relationships, our reactive stories and feelings can trap us in this type of vicious cycle.

The Reactive Cycle

It is important to see how a reactive cycle is circular.

You get triggered by something your partner says or does, and you automatically react in some way. The reactive behavior you engage in will then trigger your partner. Thus triggered, your partner will start acting out his or her own reactive behavior — which only further triggers you!

In this way, we end up simultaneously cotriggering each other, but we rarely see the full picture. All we usually see is what our partner did to upset us. We think, if he or she would only stop doing that thing, then everything would be okay again. But each person is responsible for keeping a reactive cycle going.

The initial *triggering stimulus* behavior that starts reactivity may be different than the pair of *reactive behaviors* that create a full-blown reactive cycle. For instance, on their date night, Eric's glancing at his cell phone was a triggering stimulus for Donna. Her reactive behavior was to complain, which triggered Eric to ignore. That pair of reactive behaviors — complaining and ignoring — created their cycle. If either partner interrupts the cycle by not engaging in a reactive behavior, cotriggering will not occur. If Eric had called for a pause instead of ignoring, a reactive cycle would have been prevented.

Often it's hard to say where a reactive cycle even starts. By the time you're aware of your own distress, it is already in motion. When this happens over and over, a couple will tend to get stuck in one familiar reactive cycle. This whole process is quite unconscious. To get free of your reactive cycle, you first need to identify it and see the full picture.

To understand how your particular reactive cycle operates, it's best to look at each puzzle piece in turn. Let's start with the typical *reactive stories.* Then we will look at *reactive behaviors,* and finally, we will examine *reactive feelings* and *body sensations.*

If you are in a relationship, invite your partner to read this material with you. Doing this together will give you the ability to spot your cycle when it begins, so you can step outside of it and stop being at the mercy of your reactions.

If you are currently single, use this information to help understand any reactive cycles that may have existed in previous significant relationships. This will help you see how cycles work so you can prevent them in your future relationships.

Reactive Stories

Reactive stories are what your storytelling brain feeds you to explain why you are upset. As discussed in chapter 5, the meaning-making part of your brain makes up a reasonable-sounding story to explain why your partner is doing something, what it means, or why you should be upset about it. As we've seen, these are often worst-case scenarios that result in self-triggering.

In chapter 5, we presented a list of reactive stories and asked you to check off any that come up in your head when you get upset. (See "Stories That Keep Us Triggered," page 72, appendix B, or the online workbook's "Reactive Stories" section, available at www.fiveminuterelationshiprepair.com.) Go over this list again and circle the three stories your mind comes up with most often. As we will see, our *reactive stories* misrepresent what is actually happening with our partner. In fact, believing our story keeps us from sharing our deeper needs and feelings. As we realize this, the power of our self-triggering stories starts to fade, and we are able to experience our real feelings.

Reactive Behaviors

The next puzzle piece — *reactive behaviors* — are what we say or do when we are triggered. Once a reactive cycle has started, these are the things we do that elevate each other's levels of activation and keep the cycle going — as we've seen with Donna and Eric.

As you look over the list of reactive behaviors below, they may seem similar to the control patterns in chapter 7. Reactive behaviors *are* control patterns, but of a specific nature. The reactive behavior of one partner pairs up with the reactive behavior of the other to create a reactive cycle. They form a circular pattern of cotriggering. The more Donna complains, the more Eric ignores. The more he ignores, the more she complains, and their cycle keeps escalating. These reactive behaviors are the ingredients that keep their reactive cycle in play.

A control pattern may come up anytime, without provocation, as an automatic, habitual way your unconscious mind tries to help you feel more in control. Certainly, your use of a control pattern can trigger your partner. Eric's automatic tendency to jump in and give advice instead of just listening could trigger Donna. Donna's reaction — her complaints — could then trigger Eric's reactive behavior of ignoring. And this, in turn, could trigger her even more. That is their cycle.

In the following list, put a check next to any reactive behaviors you have used when in distress in your relationship. (Or do this exercise in the online workbook's "Reactive Behaviors" section, at www.fiveminuterelationshiprepair.com.)

❑ Try to fix the problem with logic, solve it rationally
❑ Agree insincerely, placate
❑ Rationalize, intellectualize to avoid emotions
❑ Make a joke or cute remark, laugh it off
❑ Ignore, pretend it doesn't matter or you didn't hear
❑ Avoid, distance yourself
❑ Leave, walk out, move away
❑ Withdraw, hide out
❑ Act confused, freeze up, space out, shut down
❑ Correct other person, argue the point, debate
❑ Defend yourself
❑ Ridicule, get sarcastic
❑ Make insulting noises or faces, roll your eyes
❑ Talk over the other, interrupt
❑ Repeat yourself
❑ Get sullen or sulk
❑ Mutter to yourself
❑ Compare partner to someone "better"
❑ Label, judge, name-call
❑ Complain

❑ Criticize
❑ Lecture, teach, preach
❑ Pursue, push, pressure, prod, provoke
❑ Talk loudly in an anxious tone
❑ Interrogate, question, ask for explanations
❑ Try to prove you are right
❑ Attack or blame
❑ Yell, blow up
❑ Guilt trip

Now go over this list and circle your three most common behaviors — those that best portray how you usually operate when there is distress. If you aren't sure, think of how you have reacted when the three reactive stories you circled in the previous section seemed true to you.

Finally, underline the three behaviors in the list that represent what your partner does that triggers you the most. Make note of any connections you see between your three reactive stories and your partner's three most triggering behaviors. In this way, you can start to identify your particular reactive cycles.

Spotting a Reactive Cycle

Now write down your own three most-common reactive behaviors, which you circled, and your partner's three reactive behaviors, which you underlined. See if these behaviors can be paired. Does one of your partner's behaviors often trigger one of your common reactions? Fill in the following incomplete sentence for any that pair up in this way, either writing them on a separate sheet of paper, in your journal, or using a printout of this exercise from the online workbook's "Spotting a Reactive Cycle" section (available at www.fiveminuterelationshiprepair.com).

When my partner _____
[insert your partner's *reactive behavior*],

then I tend to _____
[insert your own *reactive behavior*].

As an example, Donna wrote: "When my partner *ignores*, then I tend to *complain*." Interlinked reactive behaviors can also pair up in a variety of ways, so write down any variations. Don't worry about doing it perfectly. In fact, if you find other words that fit better than what is offered here, add these additional reactive cycle sentences. In Donna's case, she added: "When my partner *avoids*, then I tend to *criticize*," and "When my partner *withdraws*, then I tend to *yell*."

A reactive cycle starts with either person. Your partner may do something that you react to, or your behavior might trigger an automatic reaction in your partner. For instance, let's say your reactive cycle sentence was the same as Donna's: "When my partner *avoids*, then I tend to *criticize*." However, it may be equally true that when you criticize, your partner tends to avoid. A pair of interlinked behaviors feed each other and create the same cycle, no matter how it starts. In other words, cycles are cocreated by both partners. Each triggers the other.

As we saw in chapter 6, Donna and Eric have opposing reactive communication styles, with Donna preferring the sword and Eric the shield. Each partner might exhibit different reactive behaviors in different situations, but they almost always trigger the same dynamic, in which Donna is the preoccupied pursuer, while Eric avoids and withdraws.

Your Typical Reactive Cycle

Now let's complete the description of your reactive cycles. Look at all the reactive cycle sentences you've written down and reverse them. For instance, Donna reversed her sentence, "When my partner *ignores*, then I tend to *complain*," so that it became, "When I *complain*, then my partner tends to *ignore*."

Reactive cycles are equally true no matter which reactive behavior happens first. Seeing this helps us see our own responsibility for creating and maintaining each cycle. Do this reversal with each pair of reactive behaviors you identified. If it makes more sense, combine behaviors to create a more comprehensive picture of a reactive cycle. For instance, "The more my partner *prods* and *criticizes*, then the more I *withdraw* and *shut down*. Conversely, the more I *withdraw* and *shut down*, then the more my partner *prods* and *criticizes*."

Congratulations! You are on your way to identifying your most common reactive cycle! Fill in the following sentences, either writing them on a separate sheet of paper or using a printout from the online workbook's "Your Typical Reactive Cycle" section (available at www.fiveminuterelationshiprepair.com).

The more my partner _____
[insert your partner's *reactive behavior*],

then the more I _____
[insert your own *reactive behavior*].

Conversely, the more I _____
[insert your same *reactive behavior*],

then the more my partner _____
[insert your partner's same *reactive behavior*].

Reactive Feelings

The next piece of the puzzle is the *reactive feelings* that get triggered in a reactive cycle. When we experience escalating distress, we fall into one of the three Fs — fight, flight, or freeze. The reactive feelings we experience in a cycle correspond to one of these Fs.

As described in chapter 1, being in the state of fight corresponds to feeling angry, the state of flight corresponds to feeling anxious, and the state of freeze corresponds to feeling numb. These three internal states actually include a range or group of reactive feelings, which can vary in intensity.

In chapter 1, we asked you to put a check next to any reactive feelings you frequently experience when there is distress in your relationship. Review this list now (see "Which 'F' Overtakes Your Higher Brain?" page 24, or appendix B). Then, on a separate sheet of paper (or using the online workbook's "Reactive Feelings" section), write down what you do when you experience each reactive feeling — that is, how you reactively behave when you feel this way. Make sure to place within this list the reactive behaviors you circled for yourself under "Reactive Behaviors" above.

Congratulations again! You now see more of what happens when you are triggered. You are well on your way to becoming free of these automatic reactions!

Body Sensations Are Early Warning Signals

As you feel triggered, you experience certain *body sensations* that correspond to your reactive feelings. As we have seen, the nervous system controls various organs in the body, and these organs function differently when your survival alarm gets activated versus when you are calm. When you are triggered into states of fight or flight, your body pumps more adrenaline, your heart speeds up, and your digestion shuts down.

By paying attention, you can detect these shifts within your body. You might, for example, feel a pressure in your chest, a knot in your stomach, or a pounding in your solar plexus. You may notice your muscles getting tight. These are the body sensations that tend to accompany reactive states like feeling frustrated or anxious.

Most people don't pay much attention to sensations in their bodies when they are upset. Their focus is on their reactive feelings and stories. But it is very useful to become more aware of your body sensations. They are early warning signals that your survival alarm is ringing and a reactive cycle has started. Increasing your alertness for telltale bodily sensations will increase your ability to stop a cycle sooner. It is easier to recover from a reactive incident when you can halt the cycle before falling too far into the Hole.

As we've seen, both Donna and Eric experience physical reactions when they get triggered. But they tend to ignore these and become fixated on their reactive stories. Stories are part of our *secondary* reaction to getting triggered. Body sensations are a *primary event* in the nervous system. They occur even before our minds have a chance to fabricate worst-case scenarios.

To learn to identify your body sensations, try this exercise. Pick the most common reactive feeling you experience. Recall in detail a time when you experienced it: what your partner said or did and how you reacted. Imagine the event as if it were happening again now.

As you replay this scene in your imagination, notice the sensations that come up in your body. Now describe the sensations — for example, as a knot in your stomach, feeling heat or coldness, a tightness somewhere, a constriction or pounding in your chest or belly, a lump in your throat, a weight on your shoulders, a heavy feeling, a fluttering sensation, a pain in your heart, a shakiness or tension, and so on.

Core Feelings and Core Fears

When we are triggered, two kinds of feelings arise. On the surface we have *reactive feelings,* but under these are our *core feelings* and *core fears.* Since core feelings get masked by reactive feelings, we're rarely aware of the tender emotions at the root of our reactions. Certainly, if we're unaware, our partner won't be aware of these either.

On a *reactive* level, Donna felt angry when Eric checked his cell phone on their date night. But what *core* feelings and fears were hidden underneath her anger? She actually felt hurt and afraid. She felt hurt when she imagined she did not matter to Eric. Her fear-of-abandonment button got pushed when she thought she was all alone and that he was not really interested in being with her. Core fears are also known as our fear buttons.

Why couldn't Donna directly express her core fears? She was programmed in childhood to believe that signaling distress simply and directly was not an option. Being that vulnerable never seemed to work for her. In infancy, her parents did not coregulate her very consistently when she cried. When she was a child, they often ignored, laughed at, or belittled her when she tried to express her hurts or fears.

Angry protest, a typical reactive behavior in preoccupied children and adults, became little Donna's way of expressing her distress. Now, as an adult, her core fears and vulnerable tears get masked by her anger — remaining hidden from Eric and probably from herself. Hearing her complain and criticize, it is impossible for Eric to see that Donna is really feeling hurt, afraid, and alone.

When we do not have valid information about a partner's core feelings, we tend to make up stories to explain the behavior we see. Our stories arise out of our own unconscious fears. So when Donna complains, Eric's reactive story becomes that he can never do enough or be enough to make her happy.

Eric rarely considers expressing his own core feelings and needs. Usually, he withdraws before even noticing these core parts of himself. This withdrawal reaction hides his softer, more vulnerable, core feelings — both from himself and from Donna.

In this way, Donna's story that Eric doesn't care is reinforced by his withdrawal and seeming lack of attention to her complaints.

If Donna had more valid data about Eric's core feelings, she might be able to see beyond her worst-case story about him. In his core, Eric feels a deep sadness during these reactive cycles. His core fear is that Donna will reject him. He fears being seen as inadequate in her eyes. But he can't let Donna know this. Such vulnerability is out of the question. As is typical for someone raised in an avoidant home, his nervous system was programmed long ago to believe nobody would respond to his distress. So his pattern is to go numb and hide his feelings. He does this so automatically that he doesn't even realize when he is upset, since being conscious of distress would just leave him feeling more helpless and inadequate.

Donna has no idea that he has all these feelings. She has the impression that he doesn't feel much, that nothing affects him. He always looks so cool, calm, and collected. But Eric's avoidant behavior does not mean he doesn't have tender feelings and doesn't care about Donna. In truth, the more important someone is to him, the more likely Eric will react this way! If Donna really knew what was going on beneath his shut-down exterior, she would realize how much he really cares about her, and she would probably want to soothe his sadness and reassure his fears.

Most of us have difficulty expressing our core fears and tears — the soft, vulnerable parts of ourselves. Like most couples, Eric and Donna often keep each other in the dark about the tender emotions they really feel beneath their surface reactions. Neither of them would ever suspect the other person was actually fearing rejection or abandonment. Thus neither partner knows that each of them has the power to interrupt their cycle and reassure their partner's fears.

In order to interrupt your reactive cycle, it is vital to understand what is at the core of your reactivity. The following lists show the typical *reactive feelings* that get triggered — and the *core feelings* and *core fears* that are usually hidden beneath this reactivity.

Reactive Feelings: annoyed, irritated, frustrated, angry, resentful, infuriated, nervous, worried, insecure, anxious, fearful, panicked, hopeless, confused, ashamed, stuck, numb, paralyzed

Core Feelings: sad, hurt, pained, grief-stricken, lonely

Core Fears: I'm afraid of being... abandoned, rejected, left, all alone, unneeded, insignificant, invisible, ignored, unimportant, flawed, blamed, not good enough, inadequate, a failure, unlovable, controlled, trapped, overwhelmed, suffocated, out of control, helpless, weak.

Reactive feelings are the typical emotional states that first come up when you are triggered. These hide the deeper core feelings at the root of a reaction, which generally boil down to feeling afraid. It is useful to separate core fears into their own list, as they are at the root of why our alarms are ringing and why we are reacting with survival states of fight, flight, or freeze. You might consider these three lists as a kind of emotional "parfait" — with core fears at the bottom, core feelings in the middle, and reactive feelings at the surface. Normally, we only see or express the top layer, the reactive feelings.

Generally, a core fear lives at the root of any reaction. Yet, while reacting, it can be difficult to identify what that fear is. The *reactive story* can offer a clue. For instance, the story "I can never get it right" often points to a core fear of being rejected, inadequate, not good enough, or a failure.

Be curious about the core fears at the root of your reactivity. Everyone has fear buttons, so welcome these new insights rather than trying to cover up your weaknesses. Review the *reactive stories* you identified earlier in this chapter, then look over the list above and identify the core feelings and core fears that might be stirring beneath your stories.

Core Needs

The most important pieces of the puzzle are the relational *core needs* of each partner — like the needs to feel respected, safe, and valued. As mentioned in chapter 1, core needs operate like air, food, and water in a primary partnership. In the attachment literature, these are referred to as *attachment needs*. It is important to feel okay about having such needs and expressing them in your relationship. Otherwise it will be very hard to feel safe with your intimate partner.

Partners need to feel that these core needs are being met. Otherwise, survival alarms will start ringing. Here again is the list of needs from chapter 1:

> **I need to feel...** connected to you, accepted by you, valued by you, appreciated by you, respected by you, needed by you, that you care about me, that I matter to you, that we are a team, that I can count on you, that I can reach out for you, that you'll comfort me if I'm in distress, that you'll be there if I need you.

Intimate partners need to feel valued, needed, connected, accepted, that they matter, and that they can count on each other. These are core needs for all partners in relationship. When these needs are frustrated, couples fall prey to frequent reactivity and cotriggering.

By recognizing what is really driving a reactive cycle, partners can learn how to reassure each other that they truly *are* safe — that they *are* cared for, that they *are* important, that they *are* good enough, that they *are* loved. This is why it is vital to see what is at the root (or core) of your own reactive cycle and to understand how all the pieces of the puzzle fit together.

Donna and Eric: Putting the Puzzle Together

Here is a chart that shows how all the puzzle pieces come together for Eric and Donna. This helps us visualize Donna and Eric's reactive cycle. It shows the core feelings hidden under their reactivity. It reveals what they actually need at those times they get triggered. Seeing all the parts of this puzzle can help them understand the real cause of their upsets and give them a map for spotting, repairing, and ultimately healing their reactive cycle.

DONNA

ERIC

Reactive Behaviors
complain, criticize

Reactive Behaviors
ignore, withdraw

Reactive Stories
"I don't matter"
"I'm alone"

Reactive Story
"I can never get it right"

Body Sensations
knot in stomach

Body Sensations
heavy chest

Reactive Feelings
frustration

Reactive Feelings
hopelessness

Core Feelings
hurt, lonely, afraid

Core Feelings
sad, afraid

Core Fears
insignificance
abandonment

Core Fears
inadequacy
rejection

Core Needs
to feel connected
to matter

Core Needs
to feel accepted
to feel valued

A reactive cycle is driven by the needs and feelings in each partner's core. But because core feelings, core fears, and core needs are often hidden beneath reactive feelings, the cycle persists. Donna's reactive anger hides both her tender, core feelings of hurt and loneliness and her core fears of being unimportant and unloved. Eric cannot see this hidden part of her, so he never realizes that underneath her angry complaints, she really needs to feel important to him and more connected with him.

Eric reads her anger as evidence for his story that he can never get it right. When he withdraws or shuts down, Donna cannot see his core sadness or his core fear of not being good enough. She never gets to see his need to feel accepted and valued by her.

All they have to go on are the stories their minds create. Believing these stories, they get more triggered. Not understanding each other's core fears and feelings, they might spend years believing their stories and playing out the same cycle.

When we develop the courage to reveal our softer feelings and needs, we give our partner a way to reassure us and help us heal our fears. Identifying the pieces of your reactive cycle is a vital step in this mutual healing process.

Identify Your Reactive Cycle

Now it's time to figure out the pieces of your own reactive cycle. To get the most value out of the following exercise, we highly recommend that you download and print the free online workbook (available at www.fiveminuterelationshiprepair.com).

As you do the exercise, you will be asked to pick words from the various lists that appear throughout this book; for easy reference, these lists are gathered together in appendix B, and they are also available in the online workbook. Familiarize yourself with these lists, which you will hopefully refer to again and again.

Many people report that these lists expand their vocabulary and help them communicate more intimately with their partner. Review the pair of interlinked reactive behaviors you identified above in the "Your Typical Reactive Cycle" section (see page 121). Use these as a starting point to understand the cycle that plays out between you and your partner (or former partner). Here are those sentence prompts again:

The more my partner _____
[insert your partner's *reactive behavior*],

then the more I _____
[insert your own *reactive behavior*].

Conversely, the more I _____
[insert your same *reactive behavior*],

then the more my partner _____
[insert your partner's same *reactive behavior*].

Now recall a specific reactive incident where this cycle of reactive behaviors played out, or you can simply recall any specific incident where you got triggered, even if it doesn't fit the cycle you identified. Choose a moderately upsetting incident rather than a really intense one. This will make it easier for you to step back and see your pattern.

If your partner is reading this book with you, pick the incident together.

The best way to do this exercise is by downloading the online workbook's "Triggering Incident Analysis" section. Print out this section twice if you are doing the exercise with your partner. If you don't have access to the workbook, then do this on separate sheets of paper. If you are single, choose an incident from a previous significant relationship or one from your dating life.

To reiterate an important point, a reactive incident gets started by some *triggering stimulus*, that is, by something one person says or does — for instance, when Eric looked at his cell phone too often on his date night with Donna. Once triggered, Donna engaged in a *reactive behavior* (by complaining and criticizing). Her behavior then triggered Eric into engaging in his own form of reactive behavior (by ignoring and withdrawing).

In the following exercise, the initial triggering stimulus behavior may be different from each of your reactive behaviors that cotriggered a full reactive cycle.

1. **Triggering Stimulus:** In one sentence, describe the specific words or actions your partner said or did that triggered your reaction. Be as objective as you can, describing what would be seen on a video recording of the incident as you started to get activated.

2. **Your Reactive Behavior:** How did you react? This might be the reactive behavior that you just named on the previous page. However, if you are using a triggering incident that doesn't fit your cycle, choose the most appropriate item from the list of "Reactive Behaviors" in appendix B or the online workbook.

3. **Your Partner's Reactive Behavior:** How did your partner react to your reactive behavior (or continue to act)? This might be your partner's reactive behavior that you just named above. Otherwise, select the most appropriate item from the list of "Reactive Behaviors" in appendix B or the online workbook.

4. **Reactive Story:** What story came up in your mind to explain the meaning of what happened? Pick the closest story that matches from the list of "Reactive Stories" in appendix B and the online workbook.

5. **Body Sensations:** As you recall what you heard and saw, sense how your body felt when you first got triggered. Notice the sensations in detail. What did you

feel in your jaw, in your belly, in your heart, in your limbs, in your throat? See "Body Sensations" in appendix B or the online workbook.

6. **Reactive Feelings:** What reactive feeling came up in you? Pick the closest feeling that matches from the "Reactive Feelings" list in appendix B or the online workbook.

7. **Core Feelings:** What were your softer core feelings underneath your more hard-edged reactive feelings? Feel deeply into your heart area, and pick one or two core feelings from the "Core Feelings" list in appendix B or the online workbook.

8. **Core Fears:** Use your intuition about what might have been at the root of your trigger. Pick one or two core fears that may have been activated. Remember, your reactive story will hold clues to what your core fears are. Pick one or two core fears from the "Core Fears" list in appendix B or the online workbook.

9. **Core Needs:** What core attachment needs got stirred? Pick one or two core needs you feared were not being met from the "Core Needs" list in appendix B or the online workbook.

Next, using the information you identified, make a chart of your reactive cycle similar to the one for Donna and Eric in "Donna and Eric: Putting the Puzzle Together" (see page 128). We recommend downloading the blank chart that's available in the online workbook's "Identify Your Reactive Cycle" section (available at www.fiveminuterelationshiprepair.com). Or draw a blank chart on a sheet of paper. Let the chart fill the page, so you have plenty of space to write inside each box; label the boxes as they appear in the Donna and Eric example and include the arrows.

Next, write your name above the left column and your partner's name above the right column.

Now, fill in all the boxes with the puzzle pieces you identified for yourself. In the appropriate boxes, enter your own specific *reactive behaviors, reactive stories, body sensations, reactive feelings, core feelings, core fears,* and *core needs.*

Finally, fill in your partner's side of the chart. If your partner is doing this exercise with you, have your partner fill in his or her answers in the right column. If not, then guess what went on inside of your partner, doing your best to complete all the puzzle pieces accurately.

Once you have filled in the chart of your reactive cycle, sit with it and consider how it works. Note the arrows between your reactive behaviors and your partner's reactive stories and vice versa. Follow the arrows and trace how when your partner acts a certain way, it triggers corresponding reactive stories, body sensations, and reactive feelings in you. Note how you then react with your reactive behaviors, and how this triggers the reactive stories, reactive feelings, and reactive behaviors in your partner.

By tracing this progression and becoming conscious of it, we begin to see how all the pieces of our typical reactive cycle fit together. Most of all, we see how the *core* elements that drive our cycle — core feelings, core fears, and core needs — are hidden under the *reactive* parts.

Discovering Your Hidden Core

Exploring the hidden aspects of your cycle with your partner can help you let go of your stories and get back to a loving place with one another. You will discover core feelings, core fears, and core needs that you may never have articulated to yourself or to each other.

If you are working together, take some time to discuss your

cycle. Look together at how this cycle has played out in a variety of incidents, both large and small.

Be gentle and caring toward each other around your core feelings, fears, and needs. This is profoundly transformative material, and we can feel quite vulnerable sharing these things. Be sure to treat the information like a sacred trust, and never use this information against each other. For instance, if you discuss it with anyone else, do so in a way that honors the trust your partner has put in you.

Once you come to know each other's core feelings, fears, and needs, you will realize that your partner does value and care about you. People do not get into reactive cycles with just *anybody!* The degree of your partner's reactivity is usually directly related to how important you are to him or her.

Remember that in an intimate partnership, feeling that one's core needs are being met is really important if you want to feel safe and minimize reactive incidents. While your early childhood experiences may have primed you to fall into a particular mode of reactive, insecure functioning, learning to speak about your core feelings and needs will help you transform reactive cycles into opportunities for healing.

As you learn to communicate from a more vulnerable place, your emotional intelligence will grow. You will see how your stories have been inaccurate. You will become less reactive. Your nervous systems will develop stronger wiring. And you will learn — perhaps for the very first time — that it's possible to create a safe, secure bond with your partner.

Couples therapist Sue Johnson has made vital contributions toward our understanding how reactive cycles operate. If you need further help to identify your cycle, see her book *Hold Me Tight.*

Chapter Nine

Agree to Stop Scaring Each Other

Donna and Eric never intended to trigger fear in each other. But whenever Donna complained and Eric reacted by withdrawing, it scared Donna into believing her story that she didn't matter to him. Her core need to feel connected would get frustrated, triggering her fear of being alone and unloved. Hearing her critical remarks, Eric got scared, too. He automatically went into avoidance and withdrawal to protect himself from his core fears of being unacceptable and inadequate and from his worst-case story that he wasn't good enough just as he is. By distancing himself, Eric thought he was trying to calm things down. But in reality, he was trying to protect himself from the intense emotional discomfort he felt whenever he got triggered.

Eric had no idea he was shaking Donna's relationship safety circuitry to the core by his behavior. He did not realize that, rather than calming Donna, his actions frightened her. And of course, in his triggered state, he was completely unaware of how much Donna valued him. To him, her criticism sounded like, "You are not a good enough partner. You are a disappointment to me." So he felt hopeless and withdrew automatically to protect himself.

At the same time, Donna had no insight that her reactions were scary to Eric. She thought he really didn't feel anything, and if she didn't pursue, they would never be close. It never dawned on her that the manner in which she was pursuing connection only scared him away.

Before they learned to identify all the pieces of their reactive cycle, neither was aware of each other's core feelings and core fears. Swept up in their reactive behaviors, they couldn't even feel their own core fears and vulnerabilities. They got so lost inside their fear stories that neither could see what was really happening — that they were simultaneously scaring each other!

How We Unintentionally "Scare" Our Partner

People don't communicate well when they are scared. So it is important to understand how you unknowingly scare your partner so you can take ownership for the unintentional impact of your actions. To gain insight into how you might be scaring your partner, answer the following questions.

For the next exercise you can transfer the information from the chart you made in chapter 8 in the "Identify Your Reactive Cycle" section, page 129. Use this chart to fill in each behavior, story, feeling, and need below. Or you can start fresh and refer to the lists in appendix B to fill in your answers. We highly recommend that you do this exercise in the free online workbook's "How We Unintentionally Scare Our Partner" section (available at www.fiveminuterelationshiprepair.com). Of course, if you are already using the workbook, your chart will be in it.

1. What *reactive behaviors* do you engage in that unintentionally "scare" your partner?

2. What *reactive story*, or fear story, might this scare your partner into believing is true?

3. Which *core needs* might your partner feel are unmet when you act this way?

4. What *core feelings* and *core fears* do you imagine your partner might be experiencing?

Answering these questions will give you an idea of what your partner's fear story is, but that alone does not reassure safety to your partner. You don't just say to your partner, "That's your story!" After you recognize how your actions have triggered your partner, then you have to reveal your own core feelings and needs in order for your partner to feel connected with you. This way, he or she will know that in the fact you *do* care, that he or she *is* important to you, and that he or she *is* good enough for you. Let your partner know what is really going on inside of you, underneath your reactive behaviors.

Safety Statement to Your Partner

After you have done the exercises in chapter 8 and finished the exercise above, it is powerful to share what you've learned with your partner using the Safety Statement script below. On a separate sheet of paper, or using the exercise in the online workbook's "Safety Statement to Your Partner" section, complete the following sentences using the information you've already identified above.

"I want to heal our reactive cycle. When we're in it, I probably trigger you when I _____ . [insert your *reactive behavior*].

"I realize this scares you into thinking _____ [insert your partner's *reactive story*].

"I want to disclose what is really happening in me when

I do this. No matter what it looks like to you, deep down inside I'm feeling afraid that _____ [insert your *core fears*].

"What I need more than anything is to feel _____ [insert your *core needs*].

"It is not my intention to scare you, upset you, or have you feel unsafe with me. If I were not in a triggered state, I would tell you my needs and my fears instead of going on automatic. I want us to learn to pause whenever we are triggered.

"So, could we pause and help each other calm down instead of continuing to react? And, would you be willing to learn with me how to repair the damage that results from our reactive cycle?"

If you are reading this book with your partner, take turns saying this statement to each other. Be sure to read your statement slowly, one line at a time, delivering each line while looking into your partner's eyes. If you have a partner who is not reading this book with you, consider saying it to him or her anyway. It will surely get your partner's attention in a new way. When you get to the last two questions, just wait for an answer. If you are single and are using material from a past relationship, imagine doing this exercise with that partner in mind.

When Eric made his statement to Donna, he said, "Donna, I want to heal our reactive cycle, and I want to take responsibility for my part in it. I realize I scare you by ignoring you or withdrawing. I know this makes it appear to you that I don't care or that you aren't important to me. No matter what my behavior looks like to you, deep down I'm feeling afraid. A fear comes up that I'm not good enough for you. What I need more than anything is to feel accepted and valued by you. I hope we can find a way to pause and reassure each other when our cycle gets triggered."

This exercise moved Donna to reach out and hug Eric. Donna then shared her statement: "Eric, I want to move beyond our reactive cycle. I want to own the part I have in it. I realize I scare you by complaining and criticizing. I know this means to you that nothing you do is good enough for me. But no matter what it looks like to you, deep down I'm feeling afraid. What's really going on is that my abandonment fear is triggered. What I need more than anything is to feel connected with you and know that I matter to you. I'd like to learn to pause together and repair the damage when our cycle gets triggered."

Hearing Donna share herself vulnerably, Eric moved toward her and gazed into her eyes, smiling softly. Holding her shoulders, he replied, "I want that, too. You matter more than anything to me. I really do just want to make you happy. So, yes, let's talk about how we can help each other."

Prioritizing the Safety of Your Intimate Partnership

When you recognize that a survival alarm is ringing underneath all reactive feelings and behaviors, you realize that reactive cycles are a sign of being scared. They are rooted in fear stories and represent our unconscious response when our core fears get triggered.

By reassuring your partner that he or she is safe, you can help each other heal from these kinds of fear stories. The first step is learning to recognize the early-warning signs that you or your partner are triggered — the verbal and nonverbal signs we identified in chapter 8. When you notice these signs, your task is to quickly reassure yourself and each other that you are safe.

As an ongoing practice, you can increase your overall sense of safety by listening to each other and by revealing core feelings and needs before alarms start ringing. When you tune in to each other and hear each other's points of view, this enables you to resolve issues in ways that work for both of you. Remember to do and say reassuring things even when no one is triggered. This will reduce the frequency of triggering incidents. Then, when someone does get triggered, you know how to quickly reassure safety.

As you understand how your reactive behaviors scare your partner, you'll also learn not to take his or her fear reactions as an indictment of you. This will make it easier to reassure your partner as quickly as possible that these fears are not real.

Could it possibly be that simple? Yes, it could! Consistently reassuring each other's safety is the fastest way to overcome reactive cycles and stay happy in love.

Pause-Calm-Repair

When you can't quite catch triggering in time, and you find yourselves in a reactive cycle, there is still a way to bring yourselves back to a safe, loving feeling. The magic formula is to pause, calm yourselves, and then repair.

We have named these three interlinked actions *Pause-Calm-Repair*. This is the heart of the Five-Minute Relationship Repair process. We will overview these actions below, and the next chapter will describe how to repair upsets.

Knowing how to Pause-Calm-Repair can shift a distressed relationship toward one of safety, acceptance, and reconnection. When practiced regularly over time, these actions will rewire your brain in a way that helps you remain calm and open-hearted even when dealing with differences or upsets.

Pause

Catch your reactive cycle as soon as you see it. As soon as you notice that you or your partner is triggered, it's time to use your pause signal (see chapter 2). Immediately stop doing what you're doing. To catch triggers early, learn to pay attention to your body sensations and feelings, the stories in your head, and how you are acting. Notice if your partner's facial expressions and voice tones are signaling distress. When you are familiar with your buttons and your typical signs of reactivity — your own and your partner's — you'll be better equipped to notice the onset of your cycle and ask for a pause.

Per chapter 2, make a habit of pausing. Establish an agreement with your partner to practice a pause signal. If your partner is not ready to make such an agreement, start pausing on your own. If you do this, be sure not to blame your partner for triggering you, and be sure your sincere intent is to reassure yourself that you are in no real danger.

Pauses can be anything from brief lulls to slow a conversation down to lengthy time-outs apart from each other. Once you get the hang of it, and you catch your reactive cycles quickly before they escalate, pauses can often be fairly brief — only a few minutes. The importance and value of pausing cannot be overemphasized. It wires into your nervous system the braking function that allows you to counter the automatic stuck-on-the-floor accelerator of your instinctual fight-or-flight reaction. Only by putting on the brakes can you change the negative direction of your communication and stay out of the Hole.

Calm

During your pause, the aim is to get your higher brain back online. Do whatever it takes to calm yourself and, if appropriate, to calm each other. Feel your body sensations. Do conscious breathing. Offer yourself positive, reassuring self-talk.

The tools in chapter 3 offer a variety of ways to calm your own nervous system. Some of them can be used during a conversation, without your partner even knowing it. Per chapter 3, start using these tools regularly to discover the ones that work most easily and effectively for you. Remember, committing to using the pause signal and a self-calming tool is a commitment to your own healthy functioning. By making this a practice, you are rewiring your brain so you can give and receive love as a secure functioning partner.

After pausing and as soon as you are calm enough, help calm and coregulate your partner using supportive touch, hugging, eye contact, soothing voice tones, and friendly, reassuring words. Chapter 4 describes coregulation in detail. This helps get your higher brains back online as soon as possible (see also chapter 14). Physical coregulation helps create a sense of safety even during the most alarming moments.

If you find you are too upset and can't calm yourself easily, request that you and your partner take a longer pause of a few hours or so. Then, do something more involved to get centered, such as getting physical exercise, taking a walk in nature, taking yourself to a place that feels friendly or safe, reading a book that inspires you, or even seeing a good movie.

One possible approach if you get really stuck is to try writing down all your negative feelings and thoughts on a piece of paper. Do this as a personal venting exercise — to release your upset feelings by putting them on paper. Keep writing until there's nothing left to come out.

Repair

Once your survival alarms are calmed down, it's time to engage in the Five-Minute Relationship Repair process, which is described in the next chapter. The goal of this process is to repair any damage that may have occurred to your trust or closeness and to deepen intimacy and trust.

Similar to the Safety Statement in this chapter, you will learn a concise, powerful Repair Statement — a script that gets to the heart of what needs to be said. During this repair, you disclose core feelings and needs in a way that is responsible, vulnerable, and nonblaming. You share what core fears got triggered. You learn how to listen in a way that is open, responsive, and compassionate. This reassuring response builds safety, trust, and reconnection. Over time, this helps you tune in to each other, be empathetic, and reassure each other that your fear stories are not accurate.

Agree to Rewire Your Partnership for Safety

Each time you catch a reactive cycle and use Pause-Calm-Repair, you rewire a little more safety into your relationship. Doing this provides you with *corrective emotional experiences*. Your brain gets better in its ability to self-regulate, and you get triggered less often.

Ironically, this means your reactive cycles are ideal vehicles for fostering emotional healing. Insecure circuits need to be activated a little bit in order to be rewired — but not overactivated. So it is best to catch reactive incidents early. The more consistently we can catch distress states and then use Pause-Calm-Repair, the more rapidly and effectively we will rewire each other for secure attachment and loving communication.

Chapter Ten

Quickly Repair
Any Relationship Rupture

THIS CHAPTER DESCRIBES the Five-Minute Relationship Repair process to repair ruptures in trust or connection and get back to feeling safe and loving. With practice, repairs can eventually be done in a very short time — five minutes or less. The third step in the Pause-Calm-Repair sequence, repair can start as soon as you have paused and calmed down. Once you are ready to look together at what happened and to take responsibility for your own buttons and reactions, you can engage in the constructive communication that will heal what was triggered and rewire your relationship for more secure functioning.

When you reveal your hurt feelings, fears, and core needs, this creates empathy and connection with your partner. When you each take responsibility for your part in creating the reactive incident, this helps you both relax, put down your sword or shield, and open your hearts to each other.

In the repair process, you each take a turn as talker and listener. As the talker, you accurately describe what triggered you, what vulnerable feelings and fears this brought up in you, and what you really need to feel in order for your fears to be quelled. In this chapter, we provide a Five-Minute Relationship Repair script to guide you in exactly what to say.

As listener, you openly listen to your partner. If you are in the role of the listener before you have had your turn to talk, this can be challenging. Try to remember that once your partner feels heard, he or she will likely be a better listener, which is one benefit of letting your partner talk first. Initially, the best practice is to take turns going first — so that sometimes you start and sometimes your partner starts.

As you and your partner learn and practice this repair process, you will discover it is simpler than you could imagine, and that it actually only takes five minutes to do it well.

The Repair Statement — A Script for Speaking from Your Core

Here is a script for how to talk about a triggering or upsetting incident in a way that can start the repair process. We refer to this as the *Repair Statement*. While it can take a few minutes or more to prepare, it takes less than sixty seconds to present aloud to your partner.

We highly recommend that you print out the online workbook's "Repair Statement Script" section (available for free at www.fiveminuterelationshiprepair.com). Use it for the following exercise and keep some blank forms handy for whenever you need to repair an incident in your relationship. The more you apply this tool on an ongoing basis to your daily life, the faster you will transform your relationship.

For this practice exercise, start by thinking of a specific, recent time you and your partner fell into your reactive cycle. Fill in the blanks to finish the sentences in the Repair Statement below.

Either use the reactive incident you identified in chapter 8 (see "Identify Your Reactive Cycle," page 129) or use a different one. For practice, we recommend you choose an incident that was only moderately upsetting. The same puzzle pieces from the reactive cycle chart are used in the script below. If you are repairing a new or different incident, then identify each piece, by selecting items from the lists in appendix B.

Finally, it is more powerful to keep things simple. The fewer words the better. So in this script, restrict yourself to filling in just one item per blank line. If there is more than one item you could enter, choose the stronger one. For instance, if you could name two core fears in the script below, just put in the one that feels the strongest.

"I'd like to repair something with you. Is this a good time?

"I got triggered when I heard you say (or saw you do)

_____
[name your partner's specific words or actions].

"A story came up in my mind that _____
[describe your *reactive story*].

"I reacted by _____
[describe your *reactive behavior*].

"But deep down inside, I felt _____
[name your *core feeling*].

"A fear came up in me that _____
[name your *core fear*].

"What I needed more than anything was to feel
_____ [name your *core need*].

"I am sorry I reacted that way and would like to take it back.

"If I could do it over again, I would have told you that
I was feeling _____
[repeat your *core feeling* and *core fear*].

"And I would have asked for reassurance that _____
[repeat your *core need*]."

The Key Elements of a Repair Statement

At first, as you train yourself in this new way of communication, use the Repair Statement exactly as scripted. Do not improvise as you deliver it — because it's too easy to slip up and say something that will trigger your partner.

When you deliver your statement, do so slowly, one line at a time. Read each line on the page and deliver it while looking into your partner's eyes. Watch him or her receive each line before moving to the next. Also, it would be ideal if you and your partner are holding hands or in some other way engaged in supportive touch, like having a hand on the other's leg. This should place your heads about three to four feet apart, an optimal distance for taking in information through the eyes. If at any point in the process you wish for another form of coregulation — like being hugged or held — you may request that as well.

As you become more confident in this technique, you can vary or adjust the phrasing of the Repair Statement as necessary for your situation. Sometimes, not all of the elements will be necessary. You can also change the order and/or insert requests for coregulation at any point.

Whatever words you use, here is a breakdown of the key elements of a Repair Statement:

1. State your intent to repair.
2. Ask permission to do so now, and if now is not a good time, set up a time that works for both.

3. Report what you heard, saw, and felt.

4. Report what this meant to you, the story that came up in you about what you heard or saw.

5. Acknowledge your reactive behavior, and apologize for it.

6. Name the fear button that got pushed in you, describing what you felt and what you were afraid of.

7. Name your core need or the need you feared would not be met.

8. Explain how you would have acted if you had been more conscious of your core feelings and needs.

9. Ask for coregulation or reassurance that your fear is not true.

Donna and Eric's Repair Statements

When Donna and Eric started using the Repair Statement to repair reactive incidents, they were amazed to discover that, no matter what their fight seemed to be about, at the root of most upsets were the same core fears and needs.

As an example, one day their reactive cycle got triggered when Eric came home late from work on a night Donna had cooked something special for dinner. Unable to reach Eric on his cell phone, Donna began to worry. She left a message expressing her frustration. By the time Eric arrived home, dinner had cooled off while Donna had heated up.

Walking into the kitchen, Eric offered a casual hello and started sorting through the day's mail. He didn't seem to notice the fresh flowers, candles, and their fancy wine glasses on the dining room table. Gesturing toward the table, Donna snapped, "Don't you even notice all this? All you care about is work!"

Hearing her voice tone and suddenly feeling like leaving, Eric didn't turn around to look at Donna, who continued: "I've been cooking for two hours, making something special for us, and now you've completely ruined our dinner. I don't even want to eat!" She started to leave the room.

Realizing by Donna's tone and the heavy weight he felt in his chest that their reactive cycle was under way, Eric quickly interjected with their pause signal, "Donna, can we pause? This is our reactive cycle." Though still frustrated, Donna appreciated that Eric was initiating this request. She calmed down a bit, and as she felt the familiar knot in her stomach, she realized she was triggered. She joined Eric in taking some deep breaths. After a minute of silence together, Eric touched her hand gently, and when she looked up at him and saw his head lowered, she offered, "I love you. We can figure this out together. Let's fill out our Repair Statements."

After taking a ten-minute break to do this, they came back to do the Five-Minute Relationship Repair process. They sat face-to-face, knees touching. Donna started, reading slowly from her statement and delivering each sentence into Eric's eyes: "Eric, I'd like to repair what just happened. I was triggered by you coming home later than expected. I had been hoping to share a romantic dinner together, but when you came home later than usual, and I couldn't reach you by phone, a story came up in my mind that our marriage isn't as important to you as your work. I reacted with the accusation that you don't care about us, that your work is more important, but deep down I was feeling hurt and alone. An old fear of abandonment was triggered in me. What I need more than anything is to feel I matter to you. I'm sorry for lashing out, and I'd like to take it back. I wish I could have just told you, 'I'm feeling hurt and scared. I think I need reassurance that our marriage is important to you.'"

This statement touched Eric's heart. He leaned closer to Donna and held her hand. He looked into her eyes and said,

"When I think about you preparing that dinner and my being late, I feel sorrow that I did that, Donna. And I'm so sorry that hurt you. Our marriage is very important to me. You matter to me more than anything." Seeing Donna's eyes begin to water, he paused and held her gaze. Putting his hand on her leg, he then repeated even more slowly, "Donna, you matter to me — more than anything else in the world."

Wiping her eyes, Donna smiled. They hugged until they felt each other fully relax. Then she said, "Okay, let's eat! I think the dinner will still be great. But wait, I want to hear you read your Repair Statement. Can we do that first?"

Now it was Eric's turn to talk, while Donna listened. He got out his Repair Statement and read it to her:

"Donna, I'd like to repair what happened when I got home. When I came into the kitchen, I was already triggered. Driving home, I listened to your message on my cell phone. When I heard your voice tone, a story came up in my head that I could never get it right with you. I reacted by growing stiff and cold inside, and I tried to think about other things. I was trying to avoid feeling anything. So I didn't call you back. But deep down, I now see that my old fear of failure was coming up in me, the fear that I'm not good enough. What I need more than anything is to feel accepted and valued by you. I'm sorry I shut you out, ignoring what was happening with you. If I could do it over, I would have called you back and said, 'When I listened to your voice message, a fear came up in me about not being good enough. I want to feel safe enough to open up and tell you how sorry I am that you couldn't reach me. I need your help trusting that even if I'm not perfect, you do accept and value me.'"

Donna was so moved by Eric's repair statement that she reached out, touched his chest, and looked into his eyes for a moment. Then slowly she said, "Eric, I feel so lucky that you're my guy. I deeply value you, and all you do for our family. I am sorry my reaction triggered you to feel like you weren't accepted and valued by me. You are wonderful just the way you are. I'm so happy you expressed your feelings. I feel so connected with you right now."

Over dinner, Eric and Donna discussed how to stay in better contact with each other during the day, so that if Donna was making something special for dinner or if Eric knew he was running late, they wouldn't wind up in a reactive cycle. Using the Pause-Calm-Repair practice helped them find ways to prevent this sort of misunderstanding in the future.

Listening and Responding with Heart

When you listen to your partner's Repair Statement, you play a key role in the repair process. How you listen and respond is a crucial ingredient of repair. Without a reassuring response from you, no repair will occur, and the injuries you are trying to heal may deepen.

As the listener, your aim is to understand your partner's experience from his or her point of view. To do so, it is important that you have already calmed yourself sufficiently and filled out your own Repair Statement. You want to be able to accurately take in and understand your partner's message and be able to respond from your heart.

In opening up and reading a carefully prepared Repair Statement, your partner is trying to describe an important inner experience to you. Be sure not to interrupt. And offer as much empathy and acceptance as you can. This helps your partner feel safe enough to be vulnerable. It also starts to heal the hurts and fears that were triggered in the incident.

Why do most of us fail in the process of listening? Usually it is because we get triggered by something our partners say or, even more often, by their facial expression or voice tone. Often we do not realize this when it's happening. So we start to explain, defend, or argue — even if only silently in our own minds. These control patterns clog up the input channels in our brains so we are not open to receive and store incoming messages.

Generally, most people are not very good listeners. This is especially true when it comes to listening to an intimate partner talk about a reactive incident. Listening in an open, undefended way may feel uncomfortable. We might believe if we remain silent, it means we agree with everything we hear. We may fear we will never have a turn to talk. Mastering the fine art of effective listening includes recognizing these vulnerable feelings and reassuring ourselves that we are safe and that we will get our turn to talk.

Whenever you think you might get triggered in a conversation, here are some things that will help you stay open and receptive. As you prepare to listen, get centered, breathe, and relax your body. Use the self-calming tools from chapter 3 to stay grounded and calm. Tune in to your body sensations, and consciously relax anywhere that feels tense. If you do get triggered, ask for a pause. Calm down. Then come back and try again.

To improve your ability to listen, keep in mind that your aim is to find out what is occurring in *your partner's* world. This is not the time to correct or dispute things you hear. Remember, you will have your turn next, and your partner will be better able to hear you if he or she feels understood by you.

As you listen, be open and curious. Don't assume you already know anything. Be like a blank slate. Put all your opinions and needs aside for the moment. You can always retrieve these later, when it is your turn to talk. Right now your goal is to listen. Every time you listen to something that's difficult to follow or understand, you improve your skill as a listener. The benefits of this will reverberate through all areas of your life.

Repeat Back Your Partner's Core Feelings, Fears, and Needs

Once your partner has completed his or her message, repeat back the last parts you heard. Specifically mention the core feeling, core fear, and core need your partner revealed. With an attitude of understanding and empathy, say to your partner something like the following:

> "What I heard you say was that you felt _____
> [repeat your partner's *core feeling* and *core fear*],
>
> "and you needed reassurance that _____
> [repeat your partner's *core need*]."

Use the actual words your partner said, leaving out your own interpretations, stories, corrections, judgments, disputes, and self-defense. Follow your recap with these questions:

> "Did I get everything you said?"
> "Is there anything you want to correct or add?"

If your partner tells you that you missed something, try again, and do not take this as a failure on your part. It can be hard to recall the elements of a message, especially one that has emotional charge. Research shows that emotional charge will interfere with memory accuracy. So be gentle with each other. Sometimes, as the listener, it takes several attempts to accurately hear and repeat your partner's message. Often our brains will substitute something *we* would have felt or needed rather than what we heard *our partner* say. Do not be surprised by memory problems, especially as you are just learning this tool.

Give a Reassuring Response

Repeating the key elements of your partner's message — the core feelings, fears, and needs — fulfills the first part of your role as an effective listener. To accomplish repair, the other part is to give your partner the appropriate reassuring response. We call this skill *responsive listening*.

When delivering a Repair Statement, your partner is revealing core feelings, fears, and needs. If you have been listening with an open heart, you will naturally want to respond in a way that alleviates your partner's fears and helps him or her feel safe with you.

The most relevant reassurance will come from your knowledge of your partner's core fears and needs. Even if your partner doesn't explain these clearly, you may have developed a good sense of what these are by doing the exercises in chapter 8. Try to target your reassurances to these core fears and always deliver your reassurances with friendly eye contact, supportive touch, and a caring, soothing voice tone.

Sometimes, our attempt to be empathetic is undermined by an urgent desire to have our partner hear and understand our own feelings and needs. That will come later when you read your Repair Statement. Right now in the repair sequence, it is *your* turn to provide reassurances of safety to your partner. Be willing to be the first one to offer empathy, reassurance, and coregulation.

Apologies Are Powerful Healers

Your offer of reassurance to your partner might also include an apology. In Donna and Eric's example, each delivered several apologies:

"I'm so sorry I hurt you."

"I'm sorry my reaction triggered you to feel like you weren't accepted and valued by me."

"I'm really sorry I shut you out, ignoring what was happening with you."

"I'm sorry for lashing out, and I'd like to take it back."

Some people find it very difficult to apologize. This can be due to early negative experiences, like being shamed when they admitted they made a mistake. Remember, apologizing is not the same as saying that you are wrong or bad. Saying "I'm sorry" in this context communicates that you care about how your partner feels. You are saying that you recognize the painful emotion your partner has experienced, and you are sorry for any behavior of yours, even if it was unconscious, that played a part or triggered it.

In most cases, the shorter the apology, the more power it has. The most powerful apology of all is to simply say, "I'm so sorry I hurt you." The simple directness of this can penetrate deeply into your partner's brain. It can wire in the faith, perhaps for the first time, that someone cares about his or her feelings. Imagine that your partner's hurt feeling is located deep inside his or her heart. Your apology is a verbal way to put your hand on his or her heart to soothe that pain. If you want to actually put your hand on your partner's heart area as you look into his or her eyes and speak, that could be even more powerful. Always keep your words simple and your sentences short.

Note that this is not the time to clarify your intentions, such as saying that you meant to help or didn't realize your actions would hurt your partner. That would be about you, not your partner. It takes things in the wrong direction and sounds like you are trying to clear your good name or justify yourself.

Your apology can be a vital part of the repair process and a powerful healing tool. It can be like applying a soothing balm to all the hurts from every significant person in your partner's life. It will start rewiring his or her brain, and your partnership, for safety.

Hearing an apology may be a completely foreign experience to your partner. But it lets your partner know his or her feelings matter to you. This will help you both develop your capacities to be vulnerable rather than reactive. Once you hear your partner's Repair Statement, and let your partner know what you heard, practice the fine art of apology.

How to Repair with Key Reassuring Messages

By listening carefully to your partner's Repair Statement, and doing the exercises in chapter 8, you will learn which key reassuring messages are most likely to address your partner's core needs and fears. This gives you a powerful way to create more safety in your intimate partnership.

Specifically, if your partner has reported core fears of abandonment, of not being important, or of feeling alone, deliver key reassuring messages that will soothe those fears, such as:

"You're the most important person in my life."
"You are more important to me than anything."
"I need you very much."
"I can't imagine life without you."
"I'll never leave you."
"You can't get rid of me."
"I'm in this for the long haul."
"I care deeply how you feel."
"Your happiness is very important to me."

On the other hand, if your partner reports fears of being inadequate, not good enough, or a failure, core needs probably include the need to feel accepted or valued by you. Soothe any such fears of rejection with reassuring messages like these:

> "You are great just the way you are."
> "I feel lucky to have found you."
> "You're the most wonderful partner in the world."
> "You're the best thing that ever happened to me."
> "You are more than good enough."
> "You are irreplaceable."
> "You are my hero."
> "I love you just the way you are.
> "I appreciate you for all you do for me and us."

Be alert for opportunities to offer your partner one of these key reassuring messages as a part of responsive listening. Keep your statements simple. Try one phrase and see if it has a strong positive impact. If it does not, try another. Usually there is a particular phrase that will sink deeply into your partner's brain and heart, and you will see the power of this on his or her face. You are aiming for the right brain, which has rudimentary language processing ability, akin to that of a two-year-old.

Couples therapist Stan Tatkin suggests that eye contact is crucial to the success of reassurance. He recommends that you look into your partner's left eye as you deliver your key message, as this may reach more directly into the right brain. Make sure you speak slowly. Watch for breathing and facial expressions as signs of how well your reassurance is being received by your partner's brain. Experiment until you find just the right ways to combine eye contact and supportive touch with your verbal reassurances.

A reassuring message is like dropping a small pebble into the lake of your partner's nervous system. Watch the ripples and notice how your partner responds. Pause for about twenty seconds. Notice if your partner seems to relax or even melt. Note if eyes water or pupils dilate. If you feel so moved (based on your partner's signals), repeat the key message again, slowly, with pauses. Repetition will help your partner's nervous system take in your gift even more deeply.

Common Mistakes in Trying to Reassure

Below are a few common mistakes people make when trying to reassure their partners. These common control patterns can actually trigger a partner even more! Be careful not to slip into these patterns while attempting to reassure.

In reading this list, you might recognize strategies you have used. Have they ever worked the way you intended? Probably not.

Explaining Your Behavior

Trying to explain your behavior to your triggered partner never works — not until you have listened responsively. You may think that if your partner understood what really happened, then he or she would not be upset. But no matter how reasonable the explanation sounds to you, it is only useful to explain things *after* you have successfully reassured your partner.

Establishing Your Good Intentions

Don't try to convince your partner that you had only good intentions. You might think that if your partner understood where you were really coming from, then he or she would not be upset, but your partner was hurt no matter what your intentions were. Sometimes it is helpful to clarify your good intentions, but only *after* you have delivered a key reassuring message.

Telling Your Partner What to Feel

Don't tell your partner what to feel. Don't suggest he or she should not be feeling something. Particularly if you have given a particular reassurance before, you may be tempted to remind your partner of this as a way to explain that he or she shouldn't be upset. You may say, "You already know that I care about you. I've told you this so many times." If upset, your partner most likely needs to hear it again, or it may be that he or she needs a different reassuring message.

It is a mistake to assume that once you have reassured a partner about a particular fear, you won't need to do so again. Do not expect that saying something once will be enough. Most of us need repeated reassurances. If your partner does not quite take in or believe your attempt to reassure, simply say it again, using the same simple words and a calm, friendly voice.

Making a Logical Case

Appealing to logic, such as trying to prove that your partner has misread you, is a mistake. It is usually used as a way to avoid your partner's emotions or to talk him or her out of them. This can be another way of telling your partner what to feel. You think that if your partner realized his or her logical error, then your partner would not be upset: "If I didn't care about you, why would I take you to such a fancy restaurant?"

Using a Tit-for-Tat Defense

A common defense is to try to show that your partner does similar things to what you have been accused of. In using this defensive reaction you may be trying to remove your partner's justification for being upset: "Who isn't late? You were late paying the bills last month!"

Switching Roles between Talking and Listening

After you have listened and delivered a reassuring response to your partner, allow a few minutes of silence before presenting your own Repair Statement. This gives you both a chance to get centered and refocused on your intent. It also offers your partner's brain space to digest and integrate the healing reassurances you offered. This is where rewiring happens. Switching too quickly between the roles of talker and listener can cut short the healing benefits of the repair process.

The talker-listener structure helps you slow down as you discuss important issues or attempt to repair cotriggering incidents. Some discussions require multiple turns back and forth between the roles of talker and listener. Make it your goal to stay calm and open as you continue to trade roles until you both agree that you feel complete.

For easy reference, appendix A presents the full Five-Minute Relationship Repair process, with scripts for both talker and listener. Appendix A can also be found in the online workbook (available at www.fiveminuterelationshiprepair.com). We highly recommend you print out a few blank scripts and keep them handy to use in your daily life.

Doing a Full Two-Way Repair Process

Now is a good time to practice using this tool to repair reactive incidents in your relationship. In the chapter's first exercise, you filled out a Repair Statement for a particular past incident. If you are reading the book with your partner, the following exercise will guide you in a full two-way Five-Minute Relationship Repair process.

Print out two blank Repair Statements from appendix A in the online workbook, or copy them from appendix A in the back of this book. Next, each of you fill in your own Repair Statements, per the instructions in "The Repair Statement — A Script for Speaking from Your Core," page 146.

Decide who will talk first and who will listen and respond.

Each of you will have a turn to present your Repair Statement as the other listens. There may be a reason why one of you should go first, or simply make a choice together.

Sit face to face in such a way that you can give each other supportive touch by holding hands, touching knees, and so on. Take a few breaths together to calm and center yourselves. Spend an additional moment sensing how the chair holds you. Gaze into each other's eyes in silence.

When you both feel calm and ready, start the process by one of you presenting your Repair Statement. As the talker, read each line slowly, delivering it while looking directly into your partner's eyes. Watch and wait to see your partner take in each line before looking at your script for your next line. If you are the listener, offer your silent presence, curiosity, and empathy to take in what your partner is saying.

Once your partner has finished his or her Repair Statement, you, as the listener, should follow the three steps described in appendix A, "The Reassuring Response," page 258.

First, repeat the core feeling, fear, and need that your partner just disclosed, and ask if you have missed anything. As you do this, take your time. The more slowly and deliberately you go, the more powerful the process will be.

Next, once your partner feels you understand his or her core feeling, fear, and need, deliver a simple apology like, "I'm so sorry I hurt you." Say this while looking directly into your partner's eyes, and wait for half a minute to see that it is fully taken in. Watch for any facial shifts that indicate you have reached your partner on an emotional level. You may repeat your simple apology to deepen its healing effect.

Finally, offer a reassurance that addresses the core fear and need your partner disclosed. This may be a trial-and-error process. The more you engage in this process, the more you will understand exactly what reassurances your partner needs to feel secure with you. While looking into your partner's eyes, offer a simple, reassuring phrase like, "You are the most important person in my life." As in the last step, wait half a minute and watch for facial signs that show you've reached your partner. You may deliver this reassurance up to three times for maximum healing effect.

Sit together in loving presence for a minute or more before switching roles.

Congratulations! You have just done a full repair process. It may have taken more than five minutes each, and that's okay. You are just learning. As you practice more, you will get better and better. Eventually, you will be able to efficiently repair triggering incidents, quickly and completely, and keep your relationship free of emotional baggage.

Initiating a Repair Process

Ideally, you and your partner will be able to use Pause-Calm-Repair whenever a reactive incident occurs. But until you have really mastered these practices, sometimes you may get consumed by reactivity, fall into automatic behaviors, and let a reactive cycle take over. Often this leads to mutual withdrawal. In this case, after calming down, one of you could invite the other to do the repair process.

It can be hard to find the "right time" to do this, especially if you both tend to avoid communicating about upsets and reactive incidents. As incentive, remember how awful it feels to be disconnected from your partner and how good it feels when you connect again through sharing vulnerable feelings and needs. Take the initiative, even after the fact, by saying something like, "I'd like to repair what happened the other day. When are you available?"

After setting up a time, you can both prepare your Repair

Statements. Then, before you talk, calm yourselves so you are ready to listen openly, repeat back what you hear, and offer reassuring empathy.

Generally, both partners will always have a chance to talk and listen, but there are a few exceptions. One might be when someone gets triggered during the process. If that occurs, you'll need a pause to calm yourselves before proceeding. Another exception would be when a reassurance is given that immediately resolves all upset feelings.

When you both feel a sense of completion, remember to acknowledge, appreciate, or physically connect with your partner.

The Best Time to Repair

When is the best time to repair a reactive incident? As soon as possible. Many of us have a hard time speaking up about our feelings and especially about our core fears. It never seems like the right time. If we let triggers slide, however, we get even more upset at the next little thing that happens.

The ideal situation is if you can address a reactive incident while it is happening but before alarms start ringing. Then, instead of engaging in a reactive behavior, you immediately reveal your core feelings and needs and provide reassurance to bring a sense of safety to your partnership. This is a skill you can develop by doing lots of Repair Statements followed by reassuring responses.

Most couples are not able to recover and repair that quickly, at least until they have had quite a bit of practice. Simply vow to repair upsets as soon as one of you realizes you were in your cycle, whether that realization occurs hours or days later.

As Donna and Eric got better at doing the repair process, things that once triggered them into a full-blown reactive cycle started to lose power. For instance, a month after the dinner incident described earlier in the chapter, it happened again: Eric got stuck at work, forgot to call Donna, and arrived home late for dinner. By the time he arrived, Donna was in a triggered state. But she was able to calm herself, and instead of reacting, she went to Eric when he came in the door and hugged him. Then, in a soft voice, she said, "Eric, I'm upset. Could you just listen for a moment and help me clear this? It will help me connect better with you tonight." Even though he was apprehensive, Eric agreed. "Sure," he said. "Let's sit down on the couch."

As they sat facing each other, Eric moved closer to her and said, "Okay, tell me."

Donna began, "You came home later than I expected tonight, and when I didn't hear from you, I felt hurt and lonely, and my old fear of abandonment got triggered. Old stories came up in my head that I am not as important to you as your work. When I'm feeling vulnerable like this, I need reassurance that I matter to you."

Relieved to hear Donna speak so directly and vulnerably, Eric immediately hugged her, looked into her eyes, and said, "Donna, I'm so sorry. You are way more important than work or anything else. You are number one in my life. I'm so sorry I blew it and didn't call. I'm so sorry I'm late. I'll make this up to you. How about I get home early tomorrow night and we go to that new restaurant you told me about?"

Donna smiled, and Eric continued, "Meanwhile, can I give you a foot massage after dinner in front of the fireplace?"

By short-circuiting her own reactive behaviors, Donna set up the conditions for a quicker repair. Eric saw the effort she was making to communicate more consciously. Her gentle self-disclosure inspired him to want to be closer rather than engaging in his reactive pattern of avoidance. Note that, since Donna averted a reactive incident, Eric did not get triggered himself, so there was no need for him to prepare a Repair Statement. Donna was able to ask for what she needed, and Eric was happy to learn what he could do to make things better again. With practice, vulnerable communication can be that simple.

Learning to use Pause-Calm-Repair is the path to overcoming reactive cycles. The key is to keep catching reactive incidents and repairing them as soon as possible.

Rewiring Your Brain with the Talker-Listener Structure

The practices in this chapter require speaking and responding in a conscious, deliberate way. They constrain what you say so that you do not just follow your automatic impulses. This may feel restrictive and artificial at first, and your brain may want to go back on automatic (to reactive communication).

However, what at first feels foreign will gradually become more natural. In changing how you communicate, you are training your brain to think in a more emotionally intelligent way. You are learning to communicate about what really happened versus what your fear thoughts tell you this means. The sooner you start using these tools — especially the Repair Statement — the sooner you will start feeling more connected to yourself and to your partner.

Each time you fill out and deliver a Repair Statement, you are reinforcing the expansion of your emotional vocabulary. Over time, as you fill in the missing pieces in your childhood language training, you learn to communicate from your authentic core, rather than from your reactive survival-alarm system.

This trains your brain to speak more naturally, using this more emotionally effective dialect of communicating from your core. As you communicate better in real time, there will be less need to repair upsets later.

In addition, speaking from your vulnerable core feels juicy.

Your ability to express feelings adds excitement and aliveness to your relationship. You both expand your ability to hold a charge, hold differences, or hold space for uncomfortable feelings — without the need to immediately discharge tension by reacting. You experience less cotriggering and more connection. And, of course, vulnerable communication is easier for your partner to hear.

Each time you deliver a reassuring response, you discover how much power you have to heal upsets. This gives you courage to address difficult issues rather than sweep them under the proverbial carpet. You are also installing better brakes into your nervous system, so you can go slower, hear more deeply, and keep a conversation out of the reactive zone.

Each time you use these deliberate ways of talking, listening, and responding, you reduce the power your reactive cycle has over you. You are systematically clearing up the mistaken worst-case stories that your mind has been generating. You see what is really in your partner's heart, and your partner will have the opportunity to more deeply know and love you.

Chapter Eleven

Clear the Air on a Regular Basis

WE HAVE ALL HEARD THE ADVICE not to sweat the small stuff. Yet this approach can backfire in an intimate relationship. We may get in the habit of ignoring small irritations and disappointments — only to discover later that we have not really let them go.

Every day most couples get out of synch, go on automatic, or generate some sort of charged material. Partners say careless things that neither seems to notice. They have reactions to minor slights. They have different needs that don't get resolved. Small frustrations can become habitual. These little things can build up into bigger issues if they are swept under the carpet or neglected because of the pressures of daily life. That's why any couple desiring a sustainable, happy relationship needs to clear the air on an ongoing basis. This chapter presents a structured tool that will help you establish a regular clearing practice.

Clearing the air with your partner can restore harmony, create deeper intimacy, and prevent conflicts from becoming bigger problems. It helps to initiate your practice with a statement of positive intentions — a signal that initiates an agreed-upon ritual whose purpose is to heal and connect. To begin, both partners review their own feelings to see if there is anything they have withheld that might be creating a disturbance or disconnection in the relationship or that led to a defensive, cold, or aggressive exchange. Any topic can be raised: perhaps an upsetting event, an unmet need, an unexpressed want, a fearful thought about the future, or a vulnerable feeling. This is then acknowledged and repaired, in a process similar to that of the Repair Statement in chapter 10.

The Clearing Practice

The clearing practice involves setting aside a special time, either daily or weekly, to speak about things you may not ordinarily feel comfortable bringing up or things you have postponed discussing for other reasons. The practice can also be used on a spontaneous basis. Partners can ask for a clearing session whenever they realize they have unfinished business.

As with the Pause-Calm-Repair process and the Repair Statement, each partner takes turns talking and listening. The communication guidelines described before are the same. Indeed, the script for the clearing practice is similar to that for the Repair Statement in chapter 10. The main difference is that the incident or event being discussed may not have triggered a reactive cycle. It could be a smaller confusion, misunderstanding, or hurt, and so not all the elements of the Repair Statement may apply. Adjust the clearing process script as necessary to suit your situation, and see the lists in appendix B to help fill in the blanks in the script below.

Here is the clearing practice script:

"I'd like to clear something with you so we can get back to feeling connected.

"I was _____ [insert appropriate reaction, such as triggered, hurt, confused] when I heard you say (or saw you do) _____
[name your partner's specific words or actions].

"A story came up in my mind that _____
[describe your *reactive story*].

"I reacted by _____
[describe your *reactive behavior*].

"But deep down inside, I felt _____
[name you *core feeling*].

"A fear came up in me that _____
[name your *core fear*].

"What I needed more than anything was to feel _____
[name your *core need*].

"I am sorry I reacted that way and would like to take it back. [Or, "I'm sorry I was not able to share this with you at the time."]

"If I could do it over again, I would have told you that I was feeling _____
[repeat your *core feeling* and *core fear*].

"And I would have asked for reassurance that _____
[repeat your *core need*]."

Since you only need to use the sentences that are appropriate for the issue you are addressing, you can vary the script as needed. Here is what a briefer version of the script might look like:

"I'd like to clear something with you so we can get back to feeling connected.

"I was (or felt) _____ [insert appropriate reaction] when I heard you say (or saw you do) _____ [name your partner's specific words or actions].

"A story came up in my mind that _____ [describe your *reactive story, core feeling,* or *core fear*].

"I need to feel (or I need reassurance that) _____ [name your *core need*]."

As discussed below, when you describe what your partner did or said, describe it as objectively as possible, without inferring motives or interpreting intentions. Keep your description short, simple, and factual. Also, when reporting what you felt, focus on vulnerable core feelings and/or core fears and not just reactive feelings (see appendix B for examples).

For example, here is how one short clearing script might sound: "When you walked out while I was speaking, I felt hurt. I felt pain in my heart. This triggered a fear that I'm not important. I need to know that I matter."

Donna and Eric Clear the Air

Here's an example of how Eric and Donna used the clearing practice. They had gone to a large party at a country estate. During the course of the four-hour evening, there was a period of over an hour when Donna could not find Eric anywhere in the house. At first confused and then anxious, Donna looked through all the rooms where the party was taking place, but Eric seemed to have disappeared. Then, after midnight — when Donna was feeling ready to leave and go home — Eric walked in from the backyard, laughing and talking with Ginny, one of Donna's friends. Donna felt a mixture of relief and hurt.

When they got home later, Donna asked Eric, "Can we do our clearing practice now? I have something I want to clear." Eric agreed, and she continued: "Okay, thanks. When I was looking around for you at the party, I felt disappointed and hurt. When I saw you walking back into the house with Ginny, I felt a bit relieved, but a story came up in my head that you would rather be with someone else than with me. When I had this thought, I felt a pain in my heart. It brought up a fear that I was all alone. I'm telling you this because I want to feel more connected to you now."

Eric immediately moved toward Donna and held her in a long embrace. He whispered into her ear, "Donna, you're the most important person in my life. I need you so much. I am so sorry you couldn't find me." Feeling her body tremble slightly, he continued to hold her until her muscles released and she took a deep breath. Donna looked into his eyes and said, "Wow, that felt great! Would you like to cuddle a little?" Eric's eyes smiled back at her with a gleam that gave her the answer she was hoping for.

If Donna had not cleared the air, if she had said nothing to Eric, her disappointment might have dissipated in time. But when a disturbance is not cleared, it is stored in the subconscious, waiting until the next triggering event. The next time Eric did something similar, he'd likely hear about all Donna's pent-up feelings in one load — and they would be well on their way to the Hole and their dreaded reactive cycle.

The clearing practice can also be used to share with your partner something that's on your mind. It can start a conversation about any topic, such as a desire you have for the future. In this instance, you are not repairing a past event, and you would not be addressing something your partner did. Rather, you might say, "When I was driving home thinking about how busy we both are, I felt anxious. Then the thought came to me that I'd love to see if we can get a weekend away together soon."

The advantage of doing the clearing practice regularly is that it keeps you up-to-date with one another. Then, partners aren't as likely to be blindsided by a list of things they've done wrong during the entire history of the relationship. If you have ever been on the receiving end of such a barrage of past grievances, you know that this erodes trust and can be quite hurtful.

Introducing Your Message

When you want to start a clearing practice, address a reactive incident, or raise a sensitive topic, it's a good idea to start by stating your positive intention for bringing this up. Here are some examples:

> "My intention is to clear the air so we can feel closer and connected again."
>
> "My intention is to repair the reactive incident that happened this morning."
>
> "My intention is to repair the misunderstanding that just occurred."
>
> "My intention is to give us a chance to communicate better about _____."

A preamble like this sets a positive tone for your discussion. It helps each of you stay open and undefended.

In addition, you may want to make sure everyone's survival alarms are calm. After stating your positive intention — and before starting your clearing practice or Repair Statement — suggest taking a minute to assure you are both calm using one of the tools from chapter 3.

You might say, "Before I start, I'd like to take a minute to calm and center ourselves. If you're willing, I'd like us to follow our breathing, feel ourselves sitting here on the couch, and get completely relaxed."

Then in a calm voice tone continue with your message or statement.

When you have finished, it helps to clearly let this be known. End your message with a simple phrase that amounts to thanking your partner, such as, "Thanks for listening. I feel clear now."

Be Brief and Specific

As mentioned above, how you communicate in a clearing practice is very much like the Repair Statement you learned in the last chapter. Be brief. Talk about only one thing at a time. Don't link multiple events, perhaps hoping it will have more impact to build a general case. Describe one concern, one need, or one behavior that triggered you. If the event was complicated, focus only on one triggering behavior at a time (starting with what happened first). Repair and clear this before moving on to anything else.

Simple uncomplicated sentences are more effective. The brain is rarely able to take in and hold onto more than a few sentences. So the more concise you are, the more impact you have. A simple self-disclosure will be very memorable, while rambling on and covering many topics will blur your message and possibly result in triggering your partner.

Be specific. If you describe an event as if it were recorded on a video, this helps you recall how you were feeling at the time. It helps you bring more clarity and more of a feeling tone to the interaction. Also, describe behaviors without inserting blame, judgments, and interpretations. Describe events the same way anyone might who saw them on a video — including your partner. If you unwittingly insert your story (whether about your partner's motives or what he or she should have done), this will create static in your communication and resistance in your partner.

If you want to discuss a general issue, boil it down to one specific event that best demonstrates the matter. Instead of generalizing, "You never clean up after yourself," you would say, "Last Tuesday you left your socks on the living room floor."

If you want to talk about the fact that your partner is often late, describe a specific incident in neutral language: "We agreed to meet at six. You arrived at seven."

A strictly factual description of what happened cannot be debated. There is no judgment, blame, or story added in. For comparison, here is another version, one that is neither brief nor specific: "You were late again! You never keep to your agreements, and it seems like my time doesn't matter to you at all. Every time you're late you show me that you can't be trusted. I sometimes wonder if you ever think of anybody else but yourself!"

The above statement is full of generalizations, stories, and judgments and feels very different from the factual statement about one incident of lateness. So stay on your side of the net, making I-statements instead of you-statements. Stick to how you feel and to the objective facts. Don't go on and on and lay it on thick. Limit your description to a few sentences at most. If you have a general issue you want to discuss, find a specific example.

Report Your Core Feelings, Fears, and Needs

After briefly describing the situation or event, describe what you felt. Distinguish between a *reactive feeling* (such as anger) and a *core feeling* (such as sadness); consult the lists in appendix B if you're unsure. Understanding this difference will increase your emotional vocabulary and your effectiveness in getting yourself heard by others. For a clearing practice, describing a reactive feeling is optional, but always include a core feeling and a core fear.

In the lateness example above, a clearing statement might sound like this: "We agreed to meet at six, and you arrived at seven. I felt hurt [*core feeling*], and my fear of abandonment was triggered [*core fear*]."

That sounds pretty simple, but it's amazing how difficult it can be to say what you feel without slipping in a story or interpretation. This is further confused by the fact that anytime you say "I felt" it sounds like an I-statement. But that's only true if you describe your own feelings. If you say, "I felt you were inconsiderate and selfish," then you have created a you-statement, or a judgment or story about what your partner has done. "You were inconsiderate and selfish" is not a feeling. It's common to mistake a story for a feeling and to slip from talking about your feelings to judging or blaming your partner.

This structured way of communicating trains you to speak from your core. In addition, it helps you distinguish between a reactive feeling and core feelings. If you include a reactive feeling, only include one and express it as a self-disclosure, not as a way to make the other person feel bad. For example: "We agreed to meet at six, and you arrived at seven. I felt angry [*reactive feeling*]. Under that I felt hurt, and my fear of abandonment came up [*core feeling, core fear*]."

Revealing soft, vulnerable feelings creates safety and mutual understanding. When you are the first to reveal a core feeling, it opens the way for your partner to do so, too. This promotes staying connected from the heart versus getting lost in your mind chatter.

An even deeper part of your message is to express your core needs. These can also be added to a clearing practice, as follows: "We agreed to meet at six, and you arrived at seven. I felt angry. Under that I felt hurt, and my fear of abandonment came up. I need your help to trust that I matter to you [*core need*]."

Do You Have a Request?

With a clearing practice, another option is to include a request. This is a specific action you want your partner to consider doing in the future. When making a request, be specific about exactly what you want. For example, you might end the lateness example by saying: "I have a request. Would you be willing to call me if you know you're running late? I'd appreciate that, and it would help me trust that I matter."

Remember, a request is only a request — not a demand. Your partner has the right to suggest a different idea. Keep in mind that your partner may not do exactly what you want, or he or she might have a request of you. Hold the view that finding a solution that works for both of you is the goal. This attitude of openness will help your request come across as more vulnerable and less controlling.

Keep your request clear, short, simple, and direct. Keep it nonjudgmental. You contaminate a request by slipping in a judgment, such as, "I have a request. Please be more considerate in the future. Call me if you will be late." The phrase "more considerate" contains a negative evaluation of your partner. It may even be an indirect expression of anger — in other words, a control pattern. Watch out for your habitual or unconscious communication patterns. Control patterns mask your true feelings and vulnerabilities, and they often set off a partner's survival alarm.

Reactive Behavior and Triggers from the Past

As we've said, the clearing practice often focuses on smaller, everyday moments, not necessarily the more serious incidents that trigger a reactive cycle and warrant a Repair Statement. However, that doesn't mean you won't sometimes engage in control patterns or reactive behaviors that you later regret. When you do, and when you can admit and take responsibility for this, it has a powerful impact on your partner. It will help your partner feel closer to you, especially if you talk about what you were really feeling underneath your reaction or how you would prefer to respond in the future.

For instance, to continue the lateness example, you might say: "I reacted by snapping at you for being late. I'm sorry. If I could do it over, I would say something like, 'I'm feeling hurt that you got here at seven instead of six. My fear of abandonment button got pushed. Now I have a request. I'd like you to hold me and tell me I matter to you. Are you available for that?'"

If you realize that your reactive behavior was triggered from an incident in your past — especially if the occurrence brought back actual memories — include this in your clearing statement. Here is how that might sound: "This reminded me of when I was young and my father would promise to pick me up after school and arrive very late. Sometimes, he'd completely forget to pick me up."

Share how this seems related to your current experience: "It led me to think he just didn't care, and I felt abandoned. This can come up now for me when someone is late." Understanding each other's past histories can be healing and usually leads to greater empathy for each other's sensitivities.

Listening to Your Partner

The clearing practice follows the same talker-listener structure as the Repair Statement. Being a spacious, nondefensive listener is important. As you hear the impact of your behavior on your partner, resist the urge to explain or defend. Pause and take in all your partner's words and feelings. Notice the sensations and feelings in your body. Are you open or contracted? Can you take a breath and calmly sit with what you hear? For the moment, put your own thoughts on the back burner, knowing you'll get your turn soon.

After you have taken time to really let in what your partner has told you, repeat back what you heard — especially the core feeling, fear, and need that were disclosed. Experiment with including more elements as you increase your ability to remember. For instance, add in your partner's triggering stimulus or reactive story. Acknowledge your partner for what he or she said. If what you hear is surprising or troubling, acknowledge this without necessarily agreeing or disagreeing with the content — at least at first.

In instances where you disagree, it is especially important to repeat back what you heard. Repeating your partner's words gives you time to center and calm yourself. It keeps you from reacting. And it gives you time to assimilate the information so you can respond more authentically.

This practice of repeating what you just heard and checking out your accuracy is called *active listening*. It is a process that couples counselors have been teaching to clients since the 1960s, when it was developed by psychologist Carl Rogers.

The Benefits of Active Listening

Active listening, the process of repeating back what you heard, has several benefits. These include the following:

❖ **Your partner feels heard.** When you accurately report what you heard, your partner will feel you are really listening. Feeling understood by one's partner can be rare, especially around charged issues. Giving this gift to your partner will go a long way toward repair and reconnection.

❖ **You both get feedback.** By uncovering and eliminating discrepancies between what your partner said and what you heard, you clear up potential misunderstandings. Plus, if there is a discrepancy, your partner may learn how to better express him- or herself, or you may learn to be less defensive and more curious about communication discrepancies.

❖ **It allows you to pause and take in what you heard.** Pausing before responding is generally a good idea. Repeating what you heard buys you time, and it helps you move beyond any counterproductive, knee-jerk reactions that might come up.

❖ **Your response will be related to what was actually said.** Often we react to what we think we heard and not what was actually said. Verifying what your partner said ensures that your response will be appropriate to the actual message.

❖ **You develop deeper intimacy.** Listening openly to each other is a foundation for deeper trust and intimacy. Active listening creates the safety that allows partners to be transparent and vulnerable.

If what your partner tells you is vague or general, or if you're not clear what is meant, ask for more specifics. This is important. Asking for specifics is different from being defensive. In order to clear the air, both of you need to know specifically what was done and what feelings got triggered. For example, if your partner says, "You never listen to me" (which is general and not specific), you would ask, "Can you tell me about a time when you wanted me to listen and I didn't?" As always, ask for more information in a calm, nondefensive spirit. If a statement or phrase pushes your fear button, notice your reaction and calm yourself. Then, when it's your turn to talk, you might say: "When I heard you say _____, I felt triggered," or "I felt tension in my gut," or "I felt hurt."

In the listener role, adopt an attitude of curiosity and openness to learning. Avoid making excuses, buck-passing, and blaming. As always, if either of you gets triggered, pause and calm yourselves before continuing.

When you are first learning to use the clearing practice, it's best to take in whatever you hear without saying anything right away. Breathe slowly and deeply. This helps you learn to fully experience the other's words and your feelings. Be quiet and notice your breath; this is especially important if you tend to get triggered easily. If you're uncomfortable, be aware of this. Embrace your discomfort consciously, and comfort yourself using a self-calming tool from chapter 3. Reassure yourself that there is no tiger nearby. Then, once you have really felt and moved through your own emotional response, repeat what you heard from your partner.

When you can listen and be with your feelings instead of reacting, you are building trust that you and your relationship can handle the normal discomforts of life. Your partner will feel safer about sharing things he or she might otherwise withhold. You will keep your partnership clear and free of baggage.

Being open to what your partner says does not mean automatically accepting everything he or she says. It means listening to and accepting your partner's perspective and letting this have an impact on you. Listening to your partner's impressions is different than agreeing with them. For example, neither partner is obligated to comply with a request. We each must decide for ourselves whether or not to make requested changes. The primary intent of a clearing conversation is to reveal feelings and needs — not to get the other to take a specific action. Nevertheless, you may hear something that motivates you to do something, and that is best done by choice.

As always, if you hear your partner express a core fear or a core need, it is generally in your best interest to respond with a simple key reassuring message. Deliver this with supportive touch, friendly eye contact, and a soothing tone of voice.

Expressing Anger Safely

Anger is a reactive feeling, not a core feeling. The way people ordinarily express anger can trigger a partner and create even more separation. In the clearing practice, we learn to express anger in the interest of transparency and connection — not to be right or to get the other to feel bad. Once we report our feelings of anger, our aim is to uncover and reveal the core feeling or fear underneath the anger. This type of vulnerable sharing almost always leads to deeper connection. When you discuss your own anger, do so with the attitude that you are revealing or "confessing" your anger and are curious about what's underneath it. You are not trying to punish your partner, be right, or teach him or her a lesson. Take responsibility for your own reactions and stay on your side of the net; this will make all the difference in how your partner receives you. When using the clearing process to discuss angry feelings, begin by letting your partner know that your intent is to get beyond your anger and to feel close and connected.

Here's how that might be stated: "I want to clear the air about some anger I'm carrying in order to reconnect with you. I'm pretty sure that once I let you know my feelings, and you hear them, I'll be able to let them go."

If you're expressing anger to a partner who has a history of conflict avoidance, or has been traumatized by anger in the past, begin your invitation to clear the air with an even stronger reassurance. Remind both of you that revealing anger can be difficult and that you realize anger is a reactive feeling arising from a core fear. Reassure your partner that your anger is not permanent, and your aim is to shine some light on your reaction in order to understand it and get past it. In this case, you might say, "I have some anger to clear with you, and I know anger is sometimes hard for you to hear. I want to reassure you that my intent is to understand and clear my anger, not to hurt you. And I imagine that this anger is a sign that one of my core fears got triggered." A simple introduction like this can make a huge difference in the other person's ability to hear you and not become reactive.

Developing Spacious Attention

The clearing practice helps you continually clear away unfinished business so you can be present to what is actually going on here and now. It helps you develop a more spacious, less reactive consciousness. It helps you see your hurts and fears more objectively — from the perspective of a compassionate witness. As a listener, you learn that you can hear needs that differ from yours without abandoning your own needs. Less reactivity about your differences leads to more respect and ease with these differences, better problem-solving skills, and more intimacy. A clear field of attention is necessary before a couple can solve a problem or resolve a difference together. Never try to solve a problem or ask for a behavior change until after you have cleared the air.

Another important lesson that comes from clearing the air is the fact that once you express a feeling, it often changes, whereas when you don't express feelings, they stick around in your subconscious and become magnified. Upset feelings come and go and need not be scary or significant. At the same time, they usually need to be expressed and heard to be cleared.

After you have expressed a painful or uncomfortable feeling, notice what you feel right afterward. Has the feeling changed or dissolved? Notice your body sensations, and see if anything has relaxed or grown more intense.

If the feeling gets lighter or feels resolved, or if you feel relaxed and open where you had been feeling tense and guarded, you are probably clear and complete.

If you still feel upset or tense, express the same feeling again, perhaps using different words, until you feel a noticeable degree of relaxation or relief. You are not clear until you feel relaxed and connected again.

Commit to a Regular Clearing Practice

Ideally, you and your partner will make an agreement to use this clearing practice on a regular basis. Decide together whether it will be daily, weekly, or monthly, and for how long. Both people need to agree on the frequency and time limits for your regular clearing practice, and it's vital to decide this in advance. Put it on your calendars; otherwise it may not happen.

People tend to avoid conflict. They fear that, by bringing something up, they could make things worse. That's why couples need to commit in advance to a regular clearing practice, so that they will not let conflicts or hidden feelings build up.

Think of how hard it is for most people to follow a consistent exercise routine. Disciplined exercise is something that does not come naturally for most people. But it's good for us. The same goes for clearing the air. It doesn't feel natural. It can seem easier to avoid what makes us uncomfortable. That's why we need to plan ahead and put these things on the calendar.

Many people do not realize they have been carrying a load of hurt or anger until it's time for their clearing session. Then they discover that they have quite a lot to clear. Most couples will find at least a few things that need to be aired if they make the time to look.

Another good reason to schedule a time on the calendar is that most people are too busy to take time to fully feel and express difficult emotions as they occur. Our lives are often so full of tasks and projects that it doesn't occur to us to take a break to talk about upset feelings or unsatisfactory communications.

Of course, clearing can also be done spontaneously (by mutual agreement) anytime you need it — in addition to your regularly scheduled time. Don't think that just because you have a time set aside in two days that you have to wait until then. When you want to ask for an unscheduled clearing session, start by saying something like, "I'd like to clear the air using our clearing practice so we can get back into harmony. Is this a good time, or can you suggest a different time?"

Designate a Safe Space

You may want to designate a special location for your clearing practice. Ideally, choose a place in your home or yard where you will be uninterrupted and where you can sit facing each other. It's helpful to do the practice in the same location every time. That way when you walk into this room or area, you have the sense that you are entering a different mind-set — a mind-set of nondefensive honesty and active listening, in which you set aside any need to prove your point or bolster your position. Some people like to sanctify or symbolically purify the space, by lighting a candle or sitting in silence for a few minutes.

Start each session by deciding who will go first. Take turns being the one who is first, using the talker-listener structure. When you are finished, acknowledge your partner and yourself for the care and intention it takes to do such a practice. Say something like, "Thank you for doing this with me."

How Donna and Eric Overcame Conflict Avoidance

As we've seen, Eric is one of those people who is extremely uncomfortable with conflict. By the time he married Donna, he had already realized that he had a pattern of choosing partners who seemed to thrive on anger, conflict, and strong emotions.

Donna, though more easily provoked to anger, really doesn't like conflict either. That's why she is reluctant to express her upset feelings until she reaches the point of being triggered. She has carried a fear that Eric would judge her as too needy or ignore her if she spoke her feelings directly, so usually she has just complained or made "helpful suggestions" (two common control patterns).

After working with the tools in this book, they recognized how they both had a tendency to stuff their negative feelings. They discovered that this was one of the reasons they often got into reactive cycles — because so many of their hidden fears and seemingly minor frustrations were not getting aired.

They decided that if their relationship were to succeed, they would each have to personally grow in their ability to communicate things they typically held back. They knew this would be challenging, but they could see how their automatic patterns were only leading them to higher levels of reactivity and alienation.

So despite their initial resistance, they agreed to commit to a regular clearing practice. They began by setting aside fifteen minutes every evening right after dinner to express their unspoken irritations, disappointments, frustrations, wants, and fears. They decided that they would each take a five- to eight-minute turn. Having a time limit helped them learn to be efficient with this practice. They also could feel assured that the whole evening would not be spent on it.

At first when Donna and Eric sat down to clear the air, they sometimes couldn't think of anything that needed clearing. But if they sat a bit longer and really got present, they could usually find a feeling, want, or need they had withheld. Often it was simply a want that had never been expressed or a previously expressed want that had not been expressed recently.

When doing this practice, they always made sure that both of them took a turn talking and that they each felt a sense of completion at the end of their turn. Otherwise, they'd restate their feelings until they both felt relaxed and connected.

Often, so much energy would get released during these clearing sessions that they wound up laughing. After a year of doing this practice, Eric noticed that he felt increasingly safe and comfortable with his own and other's angry feelings — even with the people at work who used to intimidate him. He learned that strong feelings come and go, and he learned that the best way to get them to go away is to feel them more deeply and fully and then to express them in a safe environment with the intention to clear the air.

Their regular clearing practice helped Eric feel closer to Donna and safer with her. He became less defensive and less afraid of hearing and expressing anger and other strong emotions. And he learned to look beneath the anger — his and Donna's — for softer, more vulnerable, core feelings.

Most surprising of all to Eric was noticing that it really was possible to receive another's anger, and perhaps to feel momentarily hurt or scared by this, without shutting down his heart. He could honestly say he was getting more comfortable with discomfort!

Interestingly, the more comfortable Eric was with hearing Donna, the less angry she tended to get. He was offering a sense of presence that no one else had ever provided. Over time, this seemed to calm something in her. Coming to trust that she would be heard, she no longer felt the need to escalate her expressions in order to be understood.

Remember, the aim of having a clearing practice is to get good at dealing with the little things — before they erupt into bigger things. More frequent clearing equals fewer trips to the

Hole. Another aim is intimacy — to know and be known. We may be afraid that our feelings — especially fear and anger — will appear selfish, petty, or unenlightened, so it may feel risky to reveal them. But taking a risk and revealing your feelings is an act of vulnerability. It shows your partner that you care enough to risk discomfort in order to create a stronger relationship.

Chapter Twelve

The Power of Vulnerability:
Relating Instead of Controlling

As THEY GAINED KNOWLEDGE about their core feelings, core fears, and core needs, Eric and Donna began to better understand what had been driving their reactive cycles for years. Yet insight alone was not enough to instantly overcome their reactive tendencies and how they would cotrigger each other.

Healing core fears and triggers using Pause-Calm-Repair takes repetition and practice. It's like building any new habit or neural pathway. Sometimes Donna and Eric did better than at other times. When they seemed to be backsliding, they wondered if all the work they had done was for naught. When they were successful in getting closer after a reactive incident, their confidence soared. But overall, in spite of their occasional stumbles, their ability to catch and stop reactive cycles was steadily growing.

One of their more successful attempts to reverse a downward slide occurred one evening when Eric came home and spent most of the evening at his computer. This triggered Donna's story that she was all alone in the relationship. Without realizing the early warning signs of being triggered, she broke into angry criticism:

"You are so self-absorbed, Eric. All you care about is work. You are just like a robot! I don't know why I stay married to you!"

Eric immediately felt a familiar knot of tension in his chest. The voice in his head said, "Here we go again — you can never get it right with her." As things heated up, it appeared they might fall into a full reactive cycle. But Eric was able to notice his familiar self-talk. He also noticed the tightness in his body — a signal that he was starting to react. Instead of clamming up, he took a risk and said, "I'm getting triggered. I need to pause."

Hearing their pause signal, Donna stopped talking. After a short silence, Eric continued, "I think this is our reactive cycle. Can we pause and use the tools we've learned?"

Hearing this, Donna was a bit stunned. But there was something she liked about it. She replied supportively, "Okay, Eric. I guess so. I'm triggered, too. Let's calm down. I think I'll need a few minutes of silence, but can we stay sitting here together?"

Eric agreed. So they sat on the couch, knees lightly touching, eyes closed. Instead of moving away from each other, they leaned up against each other so they could feel the warmth of their bodies. They let their bodies coregulate. Instead of believing the inner stories that were activating them, they paid attention to their body sensations. Donna could feel a familiar knot in her stomach. Eric felt a sense of heaviness in his chest.

They deliberately took long, full breaths — to help quiet their mind chatter and calm their survival alarms. Gradually, Donna noticed that the knot in her stomach was giving way to softer, more vulnerable feelings of hurt and longing for closeness. Meanwhile, Eric found that as he breathed into the heaviness in his chest, he felt a sadness that he generally avoided experiencing. Sitting with this, he saw a deep-seated fear that he was not good enough and a fear of being rejected if he got too close to anyone.

Mustering the courage to speak, Eric asked, "Can I say something now? Are you able to hear me?"

"Okay, Eric," Donna replied.

"It hurts when you say things like I'm a robot and you wonder why you're married to me. When I heard you say that, I felt hurt."

When Donna heard this, she felt encouraged. Eric's usual conflict style was to clam up and withdraw, so hearing him disclose painful feelings seemed like progress to her, and she began to calm down.

Eric continued, "When you said those things, I got afraid that you think I'm not good enough for you. That's a core fear of mine that gets triggered when I hear your criticism. I'm afraid I'm not good enough."

For a moment, Donna had to again realize how this did not fit with her story that Eric didn't care and that she wasn't important to him (based on her core fear of abandonment).

As Eric revealed his hurt feelings, she again realized that his withdrawal was not a sign she didn't matter. She began to better understand that his defensive reaction occurred precisely because she *does* matter so much, and that his fear of rejection was what had been driving his distancing.

Donna was moved by Eric's vulnerable disclosure. It was like she was sitting next to a completely different Eric than she thought she knew. Even though they had been married for years, this was a part of him she was just beginning to know and trust. It was the very part that she needed to see in order to feel safe with him.

She looked into his eyes, gently holding his shoulders, and said, "Eric, you are good enough for me. You are great! You're the most wonderful man in the world. I appreciate you for sharing your feelings. I am so sorry I said those things. I didn't mean any of it. I was triggered. Eric, I'm so sorry I hurt you. I feel very lucky to have you as my man." Eric took this reassurance in. Almost instantly, the heaviness in his chest began to lift. Tears came to his eyes. His breathing became more relaxed and natural. The couple sat and gazed into each other's eyes for a minute.

Donna continued in a soft voice, "Are you okay to listen? Can I tell you what is really going on for me when I get like this?"

Eric nodded, smiling. Donna continued, "When you seemed so busy with your work, I got frustrated and started complaining. Then you seemed to withdraw even more, and my stomach turned into a knot, and I started to see red. I just wanted to get a response, but I was so triggered that I lashed out and said things I didn't mean. I am so sorry."

Taking this in, Eric asked, "So you didn't mean it when you said those things?"

"No. Sometimes I'm so triggered I don't know what I'm really feeling. I'm desperately trying to get your attention. I guess I'm afraid to simply ask for what I want."

Eric relaxed and moved toward her for a hug. They stayed together in silence for a while, just holding each other. Donna continued, "I see I'm really feeling hurt, too, when I react like that. I get afraid that I don't matter to you, that I'm not as important as your work. And a very old fear of abandonment comes up in me. When I complain at you, I think I'm actually trying to feel a sense of connection, so I chase you. I feel so sorry that I reacted that way. You don't deserve it."

Eric felt reassured to hear that Donna's reactive criticism was not due to her devaluing him. It was actually based on how much she *does* value him. Her apology helped him realize that her reaction came from her fear that *he* didn't care about *her*.

Being Vulnerable Helps to Overcome the Cycle

Donna and Eric were learning how to interrupt their reactive cycle by communicating core feelings, core fears, and core needs. In showing their softer, more vulnerable sides, their hearts opened to each other, and they started really seeing each other. They were able to question their stories, and they felt safer than ever before.

They were building what research scientists call *earned security*. Partners build earned security through expressing vulnerable feelings and by requesting and giving reassurance during times of distress. When you communicate your needs and fears and get a coregulating response, you are finally getting the kind of reassurances of safety you missed earlier in your life. This will reprogram your survival alarm system, wire secure relationship circuitry into your brain, and heal the fears that fuel your reactive cycles.

How you signal distress makes all the difference. Insecurely attached partners resort to reactive behaviors like complaining or withdrawing. Couples who function securely communicate distress by revealing core feelings and needs.

Showing vulnerability involves revealing that you are deeply affected by your partner. You are showing how much you care. It means admitting that the two of you are connected in a way that neither of you can control. Instead of resorting to control patterns and communicating with sword or shield, you openly ask for any reassurances you need.

Securely attached partners tend to do this naturally. They learned early on to expect a reassuring response. But a great many of us were programmed to expect otherwise, so it is difficult for us to tolerate feeling vulnerable. We try to stay in control by hiding or suppressing our vulnerable feelings and needs. We seem to expect that something bad will happen if we let ourselves be soft and open.

Reasons We Fear Being Vulnerable

Below is a list of common reasons people give for not showing vulnerability. Put a check next to any reasons on this list you have sometimes felt made it hard for you to be vulnerable with a partner. You can also download this list from the online work-book's "Reasons We Fear Being Vulnerable" section (available at www.fiveminuterelationshiprepair.com).

- ❑ It feels awkward and uncomfortable.
- ❑ I feel too self-conscious.
- ❑ It is embarrassing.
- ❑ I'd be judged negatively.
- ❑ I'm supposed to be perfect.
- ❑ Real men don't cry or show fear.
- ❑ My feelings don't matter.
- ❑ I wouldn't be taken care of anyway.
- ❑ It wouldn't do any good.
- ❑ My partner would feel obligated.
- ❑ My partner is incapable of meeting me.
- ❑ My partner's response wouldn't satisfy me.
- ❑ I can take care of myself.
- ❑ I'd be laughed at or dismissed.
- ❑ I'd be rejected.
- ❑ I'd get abandoned.
- ❑ It makes me look too needy.
- ❑ It shows weakness.
- ❑ It makes me feel small.
- ❑ I'd be taken advantage of if my partner knew.
- ❑ It exposes my inadequacy and flaws
- ❑ It feels out of control.
- ❑ I need to be strong.
- ❑ I'd be giving up power.
- ❑ I'd lose respect.
- ❑ My partner would gain leverage.
- ❑ I'd feel like less than equal.
- ❑ It would be used against me.
- ❑ I'm trained to succeed and win.

❑ It means I'm a loser.
❑ Vulnerable feelings are for wimps.
❑ I'm afraid to look that deep inside.
❑ It will make things worse.
❑ It feels humiliating.

If you are reading this material with your partner, go through this list and share your fears around being vulnerable. Discuss how it could be in your best interests to engage in transparent and vulnerable communication. Take some time and reassure each other regarding any fears or blocks you may have. Tackle every fear or discomfort on each of your lists. Reassure each other that it is safe to be vulnerable in this relationship. As in the repair process, look into your partner's eyes when you speak.

It takes courage to challenge our conditioned expectations. We may fear feeling small if we admit vulnerable feelings. When we were children, many of us did not get the response we needed when we cried or otherwise showed distress.

Consider Eric's experience as a child. When he cried, nobody came to hold him. Worse yet, his parents often left the room. His preverbal brain was programmed to believe that giving vulnerable distress signals got bad results. His nervous system concluded that there was no help available, that showing feelings didn't work, and that he would have to take care of his needs by himself. As a result, instead of crying, he shut down or distracted himself with toys. These were his earliest control patterns. As he got older, this was reinforced by comments from adults about the importance of being self-reliant, acting like a man, and not being a baby.

Donna's early programming was quite different. If she cried, sometimes she got picked up and held — but other times nobody came. At times her mom held her, rocked her, kissed her, and looked into her eyes with loving adoration. But at other times when little Donna was in distress, she was ignored, laughed at, or scolded. Such inconsistency elicited deep anxiety in her nervous system about expressing her needs. So her distress signals got louder and often included angry protest. By the time she was two years old, her young brain had been programmed to believe that simple, vulnerable signals were insufficient. In order to be heard, she learned to amp up how she expressed her distress. The control patterns she adopted involved escalating her emotions — raging, yelling, being inconsolable, or acting clingy.

Being vulnerable can be difficult because most of us have past experiences where we asked for attention or otherwise signaled our needs and were either ignored, dismissed, criticized, or punished in some way. Whatever the origin, many adults have trouble feeling and expressing core needs and vulnerable feelings.

Instead of revealing our needs, we automatically go into fight, flight, or freeze. If we go into the state of fight, anger can make us feel big instead of small. Feeling big, and perhaps righteous, enables us to avoid feeling helpless and maintains the illusion of control. If we go into the state of flight, we control by distancing, perhaps trying to change the subject or getting the hell out of there. In the state of freeze, we experience an inner collapse. We react by going blank, staying in our heads, or shutting down.

It is ironic how the three Fs of fight-flight-freeze seem safer than admitting vulnerable feelings — because, in reality, acting out of these states results in anything but safety. When we defend against vulnerable feelings, we subject ourselves to suffering the prolonged agony of a reactive cycle.

The Power of Vulnerability

While we might judge vulnerability as equivalent to being weak or powerless, the truth is that vulnerable communication is one of the most powerful ways to overcome our reactive cycles and feel consistently safe with each other. When we learn to reveal our needs rather than reacting to our fears, then our real needs can get addressed.

For instance, as long as Eric's vulnerable feelings remain hidden from view, Donna will continue to believe she does not matter to him. But once she knows the fears of rejection and inadequacy he is feeling, she will let go of her stories and want to reassure him that he is good enough.

Similarly, if Donna's vulnerable feelings remain hidden under reactive behaviors and control patterns, Eric will believe that he cannot get it right or satisfy her. But once he knows she really longs to feel close to him, that she is hurting and fears abandonment by him, his stories will evaporate. He immediately wants to show Donna how important she is to him.

When we reveal our deeper fears and tears by communicating what's beneath our surface reactions, we can see what's really causing our distress. This helps us know, accept, and love ourselves. We learn to love ourselves in spite of the fact that we have these fears and often need more reassurance than we think we should. Sharing vulnerably also allows a partner to help us heal our fears so we can be present, available, and trusting with them. If we never reveal our deeper fears and tears, we never get the healing words and touch that we long for.

Communicating from Your Vulnerable Core

With these tools in mind, let's return to Donna and Eric's date night (see chapter 5), when Donna got triggered as Eric checked his cell phone. You will recall that Eric shut down, thinking he could never get it right with her. Their reactive cycle took over and ruined the entire evening.

What might they do in that same scenario after learning how to communicate vulnerably from their core? Donna might notice a familiar gut-wrenching sensation in her belly and perhaps say to herself, "Whoa, I'm getting my button pushed — my fear of abandonment button." After a brief pause to acknowledge to herself the pain underneath this reaction, she'd say, "Eric, as I'm watching you check your phone, I'm starting to get triggered. I know what you're doing is important, and I value all the hard work you do for us. But I need some reassurance that I matter — that I'm more important to you than your phone messages. Do you feel like giving me that?"

If she said this, instead of complaining and attacking, Eric's response would probably be quite different. Eric would pause to take in her words and say, "Of course I want to reassure you. You're the most important person in my life. I hate it when I do things that disappoint you. I'm sorry."

After her core need had been addressed sincerely and Donna felt she was important, they could then talk about what was going on at work for Eric and negotiate a win-win agreement regarding checking his phone. Untangling the underlying emotional issue around attachment needs ("Am I important?") from the surface triggering behavior (checking the phone) is what made it possible for them to discuss what to do in a collaborative manner.

Or, in this same scenario, what if Donna still criticized Eric, but instead of reacting automatically, Eric felt those familiar sinking sensations in his body and realized his survival alarm was triggered? He might reply, "Donna, when I hear you tell me I'm selfish in that tone of voice, I get triggered. I think it's my fear that I can't do anything right — that I'm not enough. Do you really think I'm that selfish? Hearing that really hurts. I try to be a good partner and a good provider. I need some reassurance that you appreciate and value me. Are you feeling too upset, or can you do that?"

Each time partners approach the Hole and catch themselves,

they grow closer and more trusting — more trusting of each other and more trusting of their mutual capacity to resolve issues. Using these communication tools also deepens intimacy, allowing partners to be more fully and deeply known by each other. Addressing each other from their vulnerable core helps them realize how important and valued they actually are.

Being vulnerable is an antidote to being reactive. It prevents trips to the Hole and is essential for true intimacy. We get to really know each other at the deepest level.

Communicating to Relate versus Communicating to Control

Reactive cycles are set in motion by control-oriented communication — attempts to be right or stay comfortable instead of expressing core feelings and needs. In this book, we emphasize the important distinction between communicating to *relate* and communicating to *control*. When you communicate to *relate*, you place a high value on sharing authentic feelings in the interest of transparency. You let go of the need to control the outcome. This type of communication fosters knowing and being known. Communicating to *control* places a high value on getting a predictable outcome that does not challenge your ego's defense structure. Your aim is to look good, act more in control than you feel, and generally avoid emotional discomfort. Controlling communication is pretty automatic. It's what we do most of the time.

If you want your partner to love you for who you are, you need to reveal who you truly are. This takes intention and practice. We all have a lot of automatic communication habits that we need to unlearn. Learning to relate more and control less is vital to keeping your love life fresh and alive.

Here is a summary of the differences between relating and controlling:

Relating…

❖ Seeks to know the other person and to be known

❖ Values being real, unique, and open to surprise

❖ Uses I-messages and self-disclosure

❖ Listens openly, with curiosity and empathy, showing an ability to hold and wait

❖ Is responsive to the other person's pain or fear — with empathy and reassurance

❖ Collaborates to find an outcome that takes both partners' needs into account

Controlling…

❖ Seeks comfort, looking good, and appearing to be in control

❖ Values being right, knowing what will happen, having things all figured out

❖ Uses you-messages, sales pitches, power tactics, and manipulation

❖ Makes assumptions and generalizations about the other, and believes these are right

❖ Ignores the other person's feelings and focuses on one's own needs

❖ Assumes that being open to a partner's needs means giving up one's own

Most people are uncomfortable facing their own attachment needs. We try to avoid feeling dependent on our partners, as this exposes us to being disappointed or frustrated. In a relationship, we impact one another in ways that can stir up attachment insecurities, so a partner's actions can affect us in ways that are not predictable or controllable. By suppressing or denying our vulnerable feelings and core fears, we try to stay in control and act big, when in reality we feel vulnerable and small.

As a result, we all fall into various control patterns and reactive behaviors — pretending to feel fine when we're really upset, pulling out a mighty sword when we're actually feeling weak or scared. It's no wonder we have trouble getting our true needs met. We have been trained not to reveal them!

When we communicate with the intent to relate, we reveal what we are experiencing in our bodies, hearts, and minds. We report our body sensations, feelings, thoughts, and wants as these arise. The goal is to know and be known by our partner at the deepest level — not to win, be right, or stay out of trouble. We communicate our real feelings and needs with an open heart and spacious mind. We are open to hearing the other person's response, whatever it may be — pleasing or displeasing. We ask for what we want without any guarantee that we'll get it. We accept that we will not always get the desired response. But we trust that we can survive the normal emotional discomforts of an intimate relationship. If we do feel hurt or upset, we know we can express this and ask for reassurance or coregulation. Relating involves two-way communication. There are two of us in this relationship, and our needs may be different sometimes. Yet there is an overall sense that we understand and care about each other — and that we can collaborate and find win-win solutions.

It takes considerable self-awareness to relate and collaborate. A good way to develop this capacity is to track our in-the-moment sensations and feelings. When we are controlling — in a control pattern or reactive behavior — we're not even aware of what we sense or feel. We're basically on automatic, doing what we learned to do as children to cope with not getting our needs met. When you notice that you are getting triggered — even a little — that is the time to slow down, pause, and stop engaging in your automatic behavior. Feel your body sensations and your feelings.

Relating keeps your attention where it needs to be, where you can actually be effective — in the here and now, dealing with your present situation as it really is. For instance, let's say you're upset with your partner for arriving late for dinner. This feeling is front and center in your awareness. Until it is expressed and cleared, your attention will be drawn to it, and you will not be present in the here and now. Even if you try to suppress it, it will remain stirring inside of you, so you will feel distracted by it until you clear the air. On a subconscious level, a reactive cycle is already starting. Even if you try to avoid revealing your distress, it will eventually spill out, usually causing more problems than if you had communicated it earlier. The sooner you clear the air by revealing your upset, the sooner you and your partner can get back to feeling present, connected, and safe with one another.

If you were communicating to relate, you would say something like this: "I'm feeling anger at you for getting here an hour later than we agreed." Then you would pause to notice the stories in your head, such as, "I'm not important to my partner. I always come last." As you pause to notice your mind chatter, you allow yourself to experience your feelings more deeply and sensitively. Observing your mind chatter helps you see it for what it is — stories or beliefs based on old fears and past experience. When you can notice and detach from these stories, your attention naturally comes back to the present moment. You notice your body sensations and your breathing. You realize that the story "I'm not important" belies an underlying *fear* that you're not important. You see that under your anger are more vulnerable core feelings — hurt and fear. Softening to feel this, you express it simply (remembering to stick with the data of what really happened and not your interpretation): "I felt hurt when you showed up at eight instead of seven. An old insecurity was triggered in me that I'm not as important to you as you are to me. I need reassurance that I matter to you." This is what relating looks like — brief, direct, and specific.

As you wait for your partner to respond, you breathe consciously to help yourself slow down and stay connected to your sensations and feelings. Moving slowly and observing what comes up in your awareness helps you be more present to your deeper feelings — which is the best way to avoid triggering a reactive cycle. After expressing your core need for reassurance, your body sensations and emotions will change. You no longer feel angry but are calmer and more available for whatever your partner has to say. When you express the core distress you are carrying, you feel lighter, freer, and more open; you are carrying less baggage. This is how relating works. It helps you clear the air and keep it clear.

However, your mate might get defensive and tell you, "You shouldn't get upset over such a small thing!" Then, you might notice your body contracting and your jaw tightening as your anger returns. You might also get defensive, or you could choose to keep relating: "When I hear you say that I shouldn't be upset, I feel angry." Again, you would pause and find your core feeling: "Really, I feel hurt and lonely. I need to know that my feelings matter to you. I want to feel connected with you."

As before, you would wait for your partner's response. Ideally, your partner would feel the impact of what you have said and slow down, too: "Okay. That didn't go well. Let me try this again. I was triggered hearing you say you were angry at me. I guess I started getting defensive." If your partner then pauses and reflects, he or she might continue, "It brought up an old fear that I'm inadequate as a mate — that I'm a disappointment to you. And I want to tell you, you are *so* important to me. You are the most important person in my life. I'm sorry for being late. Let's spend some time connecting now."

You pause and take in this reassurance. Then, realizing that your partner has revealed a core fear, you would look into your partner's eyes and offer a simple, reassuring statement: "Thanks for telling me about your fear of disappointing me. You are a fantastic partner. I love you just the way you are."

As this example shows, you can stay in the relating posture even if your partner becomes controlling, defensive, or accusatory. If you can discipline yourself to keep relating, your partner will eventually feel safer. And as we have learned, when people feel safe, they are more likely to be open and vulnerable and to communicate the more subtle aspects of what's really going on inside. Relating helps us become increasingly more real with each other. It helps us be more fully known, seen, valued, and trusted. And it enables us to quickly course-correct those out-of-synch moments all couples experience — without going to the Hole or suffering a reactive cycle.

The Dance of Relating

Relating is like dancing — where partners are sensitive and responsive to the moves of the other. You let go of trying to predict the next move in the dance. You don't try to get your partner to follow your lead. It's a mutual dance. Each person's self-expression takes into account what the other partner has just expressed. The dance is spacious enough to include both partners' experiences and desires. It encourages you to sense your connection to each other, to exchange real feelings and responses. It inspires you to stay flexible, creative, collaborative, and responsive.

As the example above demonstrates, relating allows for a natural moment-to-moment change in one's feelings based partly on what you hear from your partner: You feel something. You express yourself vulnerably. Your partner also responds by relating. Your feelings change. After expressing core feelings, you feel lighter. Your energy is flowing again. You get a sense of closure or completion from expressing yourself in this way.

In contrast, controlling attempts to maintain the illusion that you know how things should be and can make things go *your* way. Unfortunately, when you think you're right or that you know how things should be, your "knowing" is based on the very limited ability of the meaning-making part of your brain to analyze a complex situation. You may become stuck in a position, with a predetermined agenda to stay comfortable, play it safe, or get the other to conform to your wishes.

Remember, when you communicate with the intent to control, you are focused on getting a particular result — a result that does not threaten your illusory sense of being in control. This can lead to screening out potentially vital information or overriding your partner's input if it doesn't support your agenda or your stories.

It's important to recognize when you are using a control pattern or reactive behavior — because such controlling behaviors make it difficult for your partner to have empathy for you. Thus, you are less likely to get your needs met. When you let go of the need to control and open your heart and mind to your intimate partner, you step into the unknown. You take a risk and say what's real without knowing how your partner will respond. This leap of faith tends to create a greater sense of connection because you are risking something on behalf of your relationship. Your partner will usually appreciate this and become more open, too.

In intimate interactions, relating is preferable to controlling because it brings you into the present, it's juicier, it helps you trust yourself, it helps you trust the unknown, and it helps your partner feel connected to you. Also, most people resist a partner's controlling behavior even if they appear to be going along with it.

As you grow in self-awareness, you'll probably notice moments when you fall back into control patterns and other times when it's easier to relate. The important thing is that you look honestly at what your controlling behavior is trying to protect you from, what it costs you, and whether this actually supports getting your needs met. Then, you need to go back to your partner to repair any rifts caused by your controlling behavior.

To achieve deep and lasting intimacy, venture into what feels like risky and vulnerable territory — where you don't know what will happen but are open to discovery. True intimacy grows from dancing into the unknown together.

The Subtler Aspects of Being Vulnerable

The ideal way of being vulnerable with a partner is to *reveal* your core needs at the moment you feel these needs. This is different from talking about what you need in a more general way. Revealing means showing your need, simply and directly, as it lives within you.

As an example, let's return to Donna and Eric's date night. Before Donna mastered the art of relating, she would couch her needs in general statements like, "You should know by now that I don't like being neglected!" Using this phrasing, Donna is in her head, not in her felt experience. So she is not as connected to herself as she speaks. She is not present to what she was actually feeling in the moment as Eric looks at his phone. If she were to reveal herself in a more direct, present-moment way, she might say, "I need to feel connected to you. Can you pause what you're doing for a minute and please hold my hand?" This statement arises from her present felt experience, rather than from her control pattern of hiding her feelings and needs and giving Eric a complaint or a general rule about how to stay out of trouble. As she speaks in this more present-time way, she comes across as more real and vulnerable. She is easier to hear since she is more "all-there" in her self-expression.

Can you see how asking for what you want in the moment is more likely to get your partner's positive attention? It's very specific, concrete, and immediate. It shows your partner what you need here and now rather than simply expressing what you generally prefer. Feelings create connection. Abstract announcements create distance.

Also notice that the phrase "I don't like being neglected" expresses what you *don't* want rather than what you *do* want. It is more impactful and more vulnerable to state what you want as opposed to what you don't want. It is easier for your partner to hear and satisfy a positively phrased desire. A want is vulnerable. A "don't want" can sound like a complaint, which can be a button-pusher for many partners. More importantly, complaints usually mask our core feelings and core needs — even from ourselves!

Generalizing as a Control Pattern

Many people are not aware of how often they use generalized statements and rules of thumb when asking for what they want. Instead of a clear, specific statement of what they need in the moment, they say something more nebulous. For instance, Donna might say to Eric, "You need to be more romantic." This statement is too general. What does "romantic" really mean in terms of specific behaviors?

Speaking in general terms about your wants is a control pattern because this way of speaking helps you avoid feeling your actual feelings. You are *talking about* your desires rather than *revealing* your desires. This prevents you from actually feeling your want as you express it. It's a way of playing it safe.

You are protecting yourself by not really taking a risk and asking specifically for what you want. Asking for romance sounds like a positive thing, but what do you specifically envision as romantic? Your words may sound hollow if they convey no tangible information. Worse yet, your partner may define romance differently, which could trigger a core fear in you of not being heard.

Also, phrase your request as an I-statement. Don't say, "You need to…" Say, "I need…" You-messages create resistance because they are controlling. They mask one's true feelings and needs. Donna would get her needs met better if she said, "I feel a little vulnerable right now. I need some reassurance that you love me. My fantasy is for you to look into my eyes and tell me something you value about me. Would you be willing to do that?"

Being specific paints a visual and kinesthetic picture that embodies your desired outcome, increasing the impact you have on your partner. Speaking in specific here-and-now terms, revealing difficult-to-express needs, shows a willingness to work harder to make yourself clear. Vulnerability makes a stronger impression. It is more compelling to your partner. You're showing how much you care.

Complaining versus Wanting

Complaining is a self-protective way to talk about your wants and needs. You're not risking anything because you are not directly admitting you have a specific need in the moment. Complaining is a common control pattern designed to discharge frustration or get attention — but the attention you attract probably won't get you what you truly want.

You may not be aware that a complaint is generally a want or need in disguise. When you're complaining, you are telling someone what you *don't want*, which is a lot easier — and cheaper — than making yourself vulnerable by expressing what you *do want* with an open heart.

Remember to watch out for any tendency to complain. If you catch yourself complaining, "Why don't you ever listen to me anymore?" pause and find the want or need underneath your complaint, and express that instead. For example, you could revise your complaint to a request, saying, "I want you to just listen to me unload about my job. When might you be available for that?"

When people habitually state their needs in the form of complaints or criticisms, it triggers reactive cycles and can eventually lead to divorce. Why? Complaints mask the underlying core needs, which will never be heard by one's partner. Frustrated needs will then stack up. Complaints soon turn into angry criticism and can escalate into blaming attacks and reactive cycles. Eventually, both parties give up and disconnect.

Learn to Spot Your Controlling Mind

It's important to learn to spot the controlling mind at work, interrupt its defensive patterns, and get back to sharing our core feelings and needs.

Can you recall a recent time when you didn't ask for what you wanted? Take some time to reflect on this question. We all have such moments — probably more frequently than we realize. One typical example is keeping quiet about what you want during sex. In this situation, you might use a control pattern like minimizing your want, telling yourself you probably won't get what you want, or criticizing yourself for having this want. This type of behavior reveals the belief that "It's not safe to ask for what I want. My wants don't count. I'll be rejected or seen as a nuisance for asking."

Now, with this recent incident in mind, ask yourself: What story did I tell myself to justify not reaching out for what I wanted? What fear or belief prevented me from speaking vulnerably? When you observe yourself thinking this story in the future, remind yourself that this is one of your play-it-safe control patterns. Look beneath this self-protective story for the need you are experiencing.

As you get better at noticing your unconscious patterns and beliefs, you gain an understanding of why it's hard for you to express your needs vulnerably. Each time you notice yourself having trouble being open about your core feelings and needs, offer yourself some empathy and compassion. You are healing your past so you can live and love more in the present. Over time, you'll learn to interrupt yourself when you automatically fall into controlling, and you'll come back to relating.

Here is a simple exercise to help you get free of your automatic patterns and limiting beliefs about showing your vulnerability:

Take the situation you identified above, in which you acted out a control pattern instead of vulnerably expressing a need. Now imagine, if you had felt safe, how would you have expressed yourself? What would you have said?

Say these words now silently inside your own mind. Saying the actual words that express a deeper level of authenticity and vulnerability is good practice.

Doing this practice regularly makes it increasingly likely that, over time, you'll be able to speak your needs openly in the moment, as they occur, and without apology, justification, or shame.

Sometimes the Answer Is "No"

Realistically, we know that any time we ask for something, there's a chance we won't get it. If you recognize consciously, as you make a request, that "no" is a possible answer, then your request will likely include a sense of vulnerability. Knowing that it might be denied brings depth and complexity to your request.

As you find yourself able to handle more complex feelings — feeling and expressing your want while being vulnerable to hearing "no" — you radiate a bigger presence. You'll find yourself feeling naturally more safe in the world as a result of this bigness.

Even if your partner does say "no," it is best to stay vulnerable, feeling whatever emotional discomfort you may feel — rather than shutting down or resorting to some other reactive pattern. Experiencing your present-moment feelings helps you stay grounded in the reality of this moment. This way, by staying engaged, you can find out what your partner is experiencing and perhaps explore other options that will work for both of you. To be an effective problem-solver, you must be able to *experience what is*, including the inevitable hurts and pains of relationships.

For instance, if your partner says "not tonight" to your request for sex, and you accept the momentary emotional pain of hearing this, you might continue talking to find out what *is* available from your partner — like some other form of loving touch or connection. You might adjust what you want and spend some time together cuddling. When you learn to tolerate discomfort without making yourself or the other bad or wrong, you become free to cooperatively explore how each of you might get what you need. To thrive in a world where differing needs and views are a fact of life, it's vital that we learn to tolerate the temporary emotional discomfort associated with having differences.

The Other Side of Vulnerability

Another aspect of vulnerability is that it shows your partner that his or her behavior has a significant impact on you — that you are moved, touched, pleased, aroused, upset, hurt, or disappointed.

Being open and vulnerable in this way has many benefits. It helps your partner understand your needs. If your response is a distressing emotion like hurt or sadness, your transparency will serve to clear the air between you or help you both realize the need for repair.

If you vulnerably express a positive response like appreciation or relief, your openness will help your partner feel more safe and connected with you. When you make it your practice to express how you feel soon after your partner expresses a feeling, this keeps your attention in the here and now with your beloved — as opposed to falling unconsciously into a pattern like talking about something that has nothing to do with what you just heard.

A very useful phrase you can use to help you connect with and express feelings about your partner's message is: "Hearing you say that, I feel…" Learn to use this phrase (even if only to yourself) to help remember to pause and feel how your partner's communications are affecting you — rather than responding with something canned, superficial, or automatic.

Feeling your present-moment response in your body also brings you into stronger contact with your partner. Pay attention to the sensations in your chest and belly, and share these. Showing your partner how you feel is more vulnerable and impactful than simply saying the words without awareness of your body sensations.

Learning to replace the language of self-protection (or controlling) with the language of vulnerability (or relating) will help you heal the conditioned fears and limiting expectations you learned in childhood. By making it safe for each other to feel and express core feelings and needs, you offer each other *corrective emotional experiences*, or recurring trust-building experiences that rewire your brains for secure attachment.

Chapter Thirteen

Real Intimacy in the Bedroom

Throughout this book, we have referred to the fact that everyone has at least one or two core fears or buttons — fears of being abandoned, rejected, controlled, inadequate, and the like. It's no surprise that such fears have a way of finding their way into the bedroom.

The communication tools and coregulation practices offered in this book can also be applied to your sex life. If a couple does not feel safe together, their sex life will suffer. Physical nakedness and emotional vulnerability are linked. Couples who feel safe sharing both types of vulnerability are more likely to enjoy great sex.

When reactive behaviors like criticizing or withdrawing occur, it becomes harder to feel safe to reach out and express our vulnerable wants. For example, it is quite common for self-protective control patterns to develop when differing sexual rhythms and preferences surface. For instance, if Donna is too tired when Eric is in the mood, this difference can be misinterpreted as rejection by Eric, leading him to pull away and shut down. This may trigger Donna's fear of abandonment, leading her to start asking questions or engage in some other controlling behavior. Or if Eric's performance anxiety comes up, he may not be as open to Donna's sexual overtures. Her fear of abandonment may lead her to criticize or make "helpful" suggestions, thus further triggering his fear of failure.

To feel safe with each other in a relationship, we each need to be able to communicate our vulnerable feelings, fears, wants, and needs — including our sexual feelings and needs. We need to reassure each other that we are safe, accepted, connected, valued, and wanted. An intimate sexual relationship can provide a safe place to uncover and heal core fears. When we can speak openly about our sexual vulnerabilities, this deepens and strengthens our emotional bond.

Let's use Donna and Eric again as an example of how *not* doing this can create unnecessary pain and distance between lovers. Recall that when Donna was a little girl, her mother often ignored her when she cried loudly for what she wanted. As a result, Donna came to the unfortunate conclusion that "It's not safe to ask for what I want." Now, when she is in bed with Eric, she wants him to kiss her neck and shoulders as part of their foreplay, but she can't get herself to ask him directly for this because of how that's gone in the past. So she clams up, afraid that saying something will trigger him to shut down or ignore her.

On one particular occasion, Donna tried to override her unexpressed desire (and accompanying fear) and just enjoy the feeling of Eric's hands on her body. She couldn't stop thinking, "Eric doesn't seem to like it when I say what I like! He just does what he likes. I don't matter at all to him. He only thinks about himself." As Donna's body grew more tense, she finally erupted: "I don't know why you bother to have sex with me. Do you even feel me here with you? You might as well be doing it with a blow-up doll!" This is a good example of how frustrations from other areas of life can show up unexpectedly in your sex life.

Eric immediately rolled over to his side of the bed and grew silent. His heart was beating fast, and his stomach knotted up. His mind was racing, thinking, "This is hopeless. Why can't she just trust me and relax? She's so controlling. Nothing I do is ever enough for her."

As Eric became more distant, Donna reacted with an another accusation: "There you go into your little hidey hole like a big baby. I feel like I'm married to a two-year-old!"

At this point, Eric got up and left the bedroom. Donna's fear intensified as her reactive stories erupted about how Eric was just not that into her. As she remained in bed alone, she decided to try to comfort and calm herself using a conscious breathing technique. As soon as her nervous system calmed down, she had a flash of insight: "Oh no, we're in a reactive cycle. We're going into the Hole again. He's triggered, and so am I."

Stopping the Cycle

This awareness brought her into present time. Instead of remaining caught up in her automatic reaction, she stepped back and saw what was going on. This more aware perspective gave her a sense of inner strength, so she decided to take a risk and see if Eric was willing to repair this upset together.

Donna found Eric in the living room and said, "Eric, I realize I am triggered. I want to call for a pause. Can we go to the sunroom and do our repair process? Are you ready to do that?"

Eric turned toward her, shocked and surprised. He said, "Thanks, but I'm not ready to do that. You can't just hit me like that when I'm all opened up. I'll need some time before I feel like talking. I need a longer pause. I have to leave for work in a few minutes."

This response triggered Donna even more. She felt the blood drain out of her head and into her limbs, as if to prepare for a fight. But somehow, she stayed present to her feelings rather than reacting. She went back to their bed and wrapped her arms around her own body — giving herself a warm hug. She felt the blood pounding in her veins. She noticed the tension in her stomach — the actual physical sensation of a knot in her belly. Her mind blamed Eric for abandoning her when she was most in need.

Then, the sensation of her arms wrapped around her made her realize she wanted to stop focusing on the upsetting stories in her head. She wanted to find a way to get calm and present again. Feeling held by her own arms, she again did her breath awareness practice. Again, she focused on her breathing, sensing with her arms how her abdomen slightly expanded and contracted with each breath.

For a while she struggled to keep her focus on her breathing. Periodically, stories came up in her mind about Eric. Hooked by another story, she got upset and noticed the knot in her belly getting tighter again. She then remembered to focus on her breathing, to put her awareness on sensing her body. She liked that she was able to find a little freedom from the stories by using this breathing practice. This taste of freedom helped her keep returning her attention to her breathing. Eventually, the knot in her stomach loosened again and her mind quieted.

Meanwhile, Eric had left for work feeling upset and angry. He thought: "She thinks she can just shoot me down and then call a pause, and I'll just jump at the chance to listen to her gripes. Well, not this time. She really played dirty this time. I need to show her that she can't abuse me like that and get away with it."

Calming Down

About twenty minutes later, Donna felt calm enough to call Eric on his cell phone — with the intention of asking again if he'd do their repair process when he got home. She began with an apology: "I feel so sorry that I called you a baby and said those other hurtful things. I didn't mean that, and you don't deserve it. I was triggered. I was afraid to say what was really going on for me — afraid you would judge me as too needy. Can we talk about this and do a repair when you get home?"

Fortunately, Eric wasn't too far down the Hole, so he was able to say, "Okay. Sure. I'll be home around six."

For the rest of that day, both Donna and Eric had difficulty concentrating on work and the things they had to get done. By the time they saw each other, they were ready to heal this painful incident and get back to feeling in harmony. They could both see how hard it was to feel relaxed and clear-headed when they were in the middle of a fight.

Donna had all day to sit with her deeper feelings and was ready to talk as soon as Eric walked in the door. Fortunately, she was aware enough to see that Eric was not as ready as she was. He had a distracted look on his face. "I could so easily get triggered all over again just seeing that look," she thought, "but I can hang out with my discomfort a little longer."

Sensing that Donna was giving him some space before starting to talk, Eric felt a wave of appreciation for Donna. Within a few minutes, he approached her and said he was ready to talk.

Repairing the Rupture

They each filled out a Repair Statement (see chapter 10) and took turns speaking. Donna started, "I'd like to repair what happened this morning when I got triggered. I was secretly wishing you would kiss my neck and shoulders during our lovemaking, but I was scared to tell you that. A story came up in my mind that you don't care about me, that I'm not as important to you as you are to me. I now see this is a familiar story I play in my mind. I reacted by getting critical and saying things I didn't mean. But deep down I just felt really shy and afraid that what I want doesn't matter.

"What I needed more than anything was to feel cared for and connected with you. I'm so sorry I said those hurtful things. If I had it to do over, I would tell you what I was wanting — instead of hiding my wants and hoping you would figure it out. I would have told you, 'I'm feeling kind of shy right now about letting you know what I want. I love it when you kiss my neck and shoulders. That turns me on when you do that.' That's what I wish I had said. I will try to be more courageous in the future and let you know what is really going on inside of me."

Hearing this vulnerable disclosure from Donna, Eric felt relieved. "When I hear you talk that way to me, I feel close to you. And it's a turn on! Honey, I want to give you what you want. Please trust this. I care very much about you. You are the most important person in the world to me."

Then Eric read his Repair Statement: "This morning I was very hurt by what you said. It triggered my 'I'm not good enough' button — my fear that I can never get it right or please you. That's the story I go into — that I can't do anything right, that I'm inadequate. Then I started into my 'I'll show her she can't treat me that way' pattern. I reacted by distancing from you. I'm so sorry. If I had it to do over, after hearing your words, I would not just walk away. I wish I had told you, 'Hearing you say that, I'm triggered. Underneath that, I feel hurt and afraid. It's my fear of not being good enough. Help me out here. I want to hear what you want from me — without the anger and criticism. I need to hear specifically what you want.' I really do want to know what pleases you, Donna. I want to learn to love you in all the ways that feel good to you."

Hearing this, Donna started sobbing. She said, "Wow. Thank you. Hearing that feels so good. I seem to need so much reassurance that my sexual desires are not a bother to you. I am very sorry that I said those nasty words to you instead of telling you what I want. This is a powerful insight for me. I see how quickly I react from fear when I am not getting what I want. Thank you for doing this work with me and for being such a great partner."

This incident, and the happy way it ended, illustrates some important lessons about revealing sexual vulnerability and the importance of doing repair work. Not only does this repair work bring partners closer together, it also helps heal the fears that lead to triggering. It's as if each time we successfully recover and repair, we feel stronger and more courageous about speaking honestly in the future, trusting that if things go wrong, we have a way to repair the damage.

Another lesson has to do with sharing feelings and wants during sex: If you're wishing and hoping your partner will read your mind, you're in your head instead of in your body or your heart. The more you indulge your mind chatter, the further out of touch you get — from yourself and from your partner. As soon as you become aware that one of your control patterns is taking over, reveal this to your partner in a sensitive, vulnerable way. This will get you back into present time — so you can feel your feelings and ask for what you want.

Body Sensations and Healing Touch

All too often partners suffer in silence, holding on to some ideal picture of what sexual intimacy should look like. When partners can stay open to what they truly feel and want, instead of getting distracted by stories and ideas, then real connection is possible. But real connection may also bring unexpected growing pains. As Donna started asking for the type of sexual loving she desired, Eric's fears of inadequacy would occasionally be triggered, even by vulnerable requests. For a while, Eric hid his reactions, but eventually his performance anxiety began to affect his actual performance. With increasing frequency, as Donna asked for something, Eric would start losing his erection. This triggered Donna's fears that he found her too needy and no longer enjoyed being close to her.

As this situation progressed, something unfortunate happened: If Donna voiced anything akin to frustration, Eric would shut down, too ashamed to voice his fear of inadequacy in an honest, vulnerable way. Eric thought that if he confessed his fear, he would be even more unattractive to Donna than he was already feeling. He knew he was unhappy with the situation, but he felt hopeless to change things, so he tried to go through the motions, hoping things would magically improve. But one night, Eric broke his silence: "Honey, I need to pause. I'm getting anxious, like I can't do it right." His voice faltered and he looked away, embarrassed.

Because they had repaired their reactive cycle enough times before, Donna immediately recognized that Eric's fear of not being good enough had been triggered. She put her hand on Eric's chest near his heart and waited for him to look back at her. Then she said softly, "Eric, I love how you make me feel. You're my guy. What's going on inside you, honey?"

After a moment, Eric took a big breath. Taking in Donna's reassurance, he opened up and said, "I don't know. Something triggers me when you ask for these new ways you want to be touched. I start worrying I can't really make you happy. I start feeling this tension in the pit of my stomach, and…" Eric's voice trailed off. Donna, moved by this tender revelation, felt a genuine impulse to reassure him: "Please don't think I'm being critical of you, Eric. I understand how you might feel those things. And I want you to know that you do make me happy. I love everything you do. Your kisses and your touch feel so wonderful. I really want you to hear this. I am totally happy that you're my man." She paused so he could take this in, then asked, "Do you still have that feeling in your stomach?"

Eric said, "Yeah. It's like a fist in my belly, all tight."

"Can you show me where you feel that fist? I just want to put my hand there. Would that be alright with you?"

Eric took her hand and guided it onto his belly, keeping his hand on top of hers. Then she said, "Let's just be with this together for a while, sweetheart, and see what happens." Eric closed his eyes. After a few minutes, he opened his eyes and looked into Donna's eyes: "It's starting to loosen up."

Holding his gaze, she said, "Good. Can we just stay with it some more. I just want to be with you, whatever you feel, Eric. I'm here with you, honey." After a few minutes Donna felt him relax and take a deeper breath, and then he said, "It just changed. It's like the warmth of your hand has melted the tension away. I feel so close to you right now."

In the bedroom, just like everywhere else, vulnerable expression and open-hearted listening can prevent and heal reactive cycles. In this example, Donna helped Eric using a technique called Sense-Feel-Heal, which is described in the next chapter. There are no more powerful ways to repair ruptures than coregulation, using touch, eye contact, and simple reassuring messages. As we learn to embrace whatever arises in us, our lovemaking supports deeper trust and intimacy.

Chapter Fourteen

Sense, Feel, and Deeply Heal

BODY SENSATIONS are the most direct way to know what is happening in your nervous system. If you feel safe, happy, or calm, you will feel corresponding sensations in your chest or belly. When you are upset, you will feel upset in your body, too. When your survival alarm gets triggered, body functions alter.

Learning to be aware of your body sensations offers you access to largely unconscious right brain processes — emotional states, relationship triggers, and the movement of energy in your body. You have seen how your vital organs are affected when your nervous system gets triggered into states of fight, flight, or freeze. As adrenaline streams through your body, your heart rate speeds up. Your breathing shifts. Your digestion is disrupted. Noticing bodily changes like these gives you the ability to recognize when your survival alarm is activated so you can calm your nervous system immediately.

This chapter presents a sensory awareness practice that can be used either at the first signs of triggering or sometime later. This practice helps you heal old patterns in your nervous system.

It involves tracking your body sensations and describing these to your partner or to someone you trust.

We call this practice *Sense-Feel-Heal*. Drawing from the latest findings in brain science and trauma healing, this practice involves two partners sitting together and focusing on one person's triggered reaction by tracking the upset person's moment-to-moment sensations. One partner plays the role of guide for the other. The guide assists the triggered partner by asking questions designed to increase sensitivity to body sensations. It is important to learn how to focus directly on what is happening in our nervous systems when we are upset. This enables us to bypass our fear stories and stay present to what is actually happening.

As with the talker-listener structure, each partner takes a turn in each role — the roles of guide and of the one being guided. You would use this process after a reactive incident or during one if you catch your reactivity quickly — before you are too activated. We saw an example of this at the end of chapter 13, where Donna helped Eric explore his sexual performance anxiety. With Donna's help, Eric was able to notice his body sensations as they were happening, release the tension in his body, and become more present as she offered him supportive, coregulatory touch.

Sense-Feel-Heal offers you a way to transform stuck or charged energies by giving these your open-hearted attention. Whether you use it during or after a reactive incident, note that you need to be fairly calm in order to do this effectively. Often it is best not to talk too much when you are highly activated, so make sure to pause before beginning. Then you can use it to further calm yourself as well as to deepen your self-awareness in preparation for filling out your Repair Statements.

Either partner may initiate the process. To initiate a Sense-Feel-Heal session, you might say something like:

"I'd like to do Sense-Feel-Heal with this upset. Are you
willing to guide me?"

"Are you interested in doing Sense-Feel-Heal around
what happened?"

"While we were taking our time-out apart, I realized
my upset had a lot to do with core fears I've carried
around since childhood. I'd like to do a Sense-Feel-
Heal on those buttons. Are you available to be my
guide anytime soon?"

Guiding Your Partner to Track Body Sensations

Generally this process is done sitting face to face. As the guide,
start by asking your partner how close is optimal for you to sit.
Then invite your partner to settle in and feel how the chair holds
him or her. When ready, you ask questions to help your partner
focus on the body sensations that arise as your partner recalls the
triggering incident (past or present). Then you ask questions and
guide your partner to experience and explore these sensations
with an attitude of compassionate curiosity. As sensations are reported, you might also offer supportive touch.

The following is a set of questions that you can ask. Sometimes you might repeat a question — particularly if your intuition tells you that this question is helping your partner go more
deeply into experiencing body sensations.

If your partner is still actively triggered, or is still in the process of calming down after a reactive incident, you would start
by asking, "As you tune in to your body sensations, what are you
aware of right now?"

If you are working with a recent, but not currently active, incident, allow your partner to describe it enough to start feeling a bit
activated. Ask, "As you recall this incident, see if you can bring back
the memory of what was said or done that triggered you. What do

you recall? Now, as you tune in to your body sensations, what are you aware of right now?" Remember that your main goal is to help your partner move from *talking about the event* to describing the set of *body sensations that arise now* as he or she recalls it.

If your partner reports several different sensations, ask your partner to allow one of these sensations to emerge to the foreground. Once your partner finds one sensation to focus on, invite your partner to explore the sensation with an attitude of loving curiosity. Ask about various properties of the sensation, using the following questions:

1. "Where in your body do you feel this sensation?"
2. "How big is it?"
3. "Does it have a shape?"
4. "Do you notice its weight? Is it light or heavy?"
5. "Do you notice its temperature? Is it warm or cool?"
6. "Do you notice its density? Is it solid, fluid, or airy?"
7. "Does it have any pressure with it?" (If it does, ask, "Is the direction inward, outward, up, or down?")
8. "Is it still or moving?" (If it is, ask, "How fast? In what direction?")

Go slowly. Allow about fifteen seconds for each question. This helps your partner slow down and get more fully in touch with what is happening. If your partner does not seem to have an answer to a particular question, move on to the next question.

Once a sensation is identified and experienced, ask a final question to encourage your partner to embrace and stay with the sensation: "Are you willing to stay with what you feel for a few more moments? Let's just see what happens next..."

At this point, as guide, pause and allow your partner to be in silent contact with his or her inner experience. After about a minute, return to the first question: "What are you aware of in your body right now?"

Then slowly repeat those questions that seemed most meaningful to your partner. Often, a sensation will shift. It may seem to grow smaller or larger, heavier or lighter, cooler or warmer. Or a feeling, image, or memory may emerge.

If a sensation seems to be shifting, repeat the question, "What do you notice now?" Pause to allow your partner to sense what happens next. Anytime a shift is reported, ask about it and pause, letting your partner be with that sensation. Be open to what happens next.

If the sensation seems to settle down, soften, or relax, ask your partner to be with this for a while longer. Then ask if the process feels complete. If your partner reports feeling complete, notice the facial expression and voice tone accompanying this report. Notice if eye contact is present, if vocalizations sound effortless, and if the body looks relaxed. These would be signs of a natural completion of the process.

If your partner reports getting images or stories, you may inquire about these using the same body-awareness questions. The aim is to help your partner focus on the body sensations connected with these images or stories. When emotionally charged thoughts, memories, or images come up, ask: "As you say these words, what do you notice in your body?" In the case of an image or a memory, ask, "As you see this image in your mind's eye, what do you notice in your body?" Then continue with the other questions as appropriate.

Adding Supportive Touch

If the tension level or intensity of your partner's body sensations remains static or increases, you might offer supportive touch. This is one of the most powerful ways we can coregulate someone's nervous system.

In Sense-Feel-Heal, you may engage in supportive touch in a

variety of ways. Experiment and use whatever provides the strongest feeling of safety. You might start by touching your partner in neutral areas that generally feel supportive to most people — on the forearm, shoulder, or upper back. Or you may already know the areas that help your partner feel safe. The best type of touch is steady contact rather than massaging, patting, or stroking. Ideally, have the palm of your hand make solid contact with your partner's body. Ask for feedback on how supportive your touch feels. Ask if your palm is located in just the right place to feel the most supportive to your partner.

Another form of contact is to put your hand on top of (or behind) where the triggered sensations are located in your partner's body. For instance, if chest tension is reported, you could place your palm on top of your partner's chest, or behind it, on your partner's back. Ask for help to put your hand in just the right place. Experiment with using both hands at once, so the location of your partner's tension is sandwiched between your hands — one in back and the other in front.

As guide, you may also invite your partner to shift positions — such as to lie down and put his or her head in your lap to receive supportive touch. As always, ask about the best place to put your hand. In this position, you can also offer loving eye contact, so your partner can look up at you from time to time if desired.

Be sure that you are both physically comfortable when you position yourselves for supportive touch. If either of you is uncomfortable, the process will not work as well.

Attitudes That Support Healing

The Sense-Feel-Heal process is about tracking the movement of energy in the body with an attitude of curiosity and discovery. In guiding your partner, you need to be calm and curious. Schedule Sense-Feel-Heal at a time when you feel clear and centered. Do not try to guide your partner if you have stored-up feelings or judgmental thoughts.

When you are on the receiving end of this process, the questions your guide asks are designed to help you focus on your body sensations. There are no right answers to these questions. If you even get a vague sense of a bodily sensation, just go with it. The point is to notice and report whatever shows up in your body and to let go of the stories and interpretations in your mind. For example, if you feel tightness in your stomach or throat, you might say, "I have a knot in my stomach" or a "lump in my throat." Let go of thoughts such as, "I shouldn't be reacting this strongly." The goal is to get better at experiencing *what is*.

The Sense-Feel-Heal process gives us a different way of experiencing potentially uncomfortable sensations or emotions by encouraging an attitude of spaciousness and curiosity. Allow plenty of time for feelings to change and move however they will. In moving beyond the mental level and focusing on sensations, you must continually suspend judgment about whether what you're feeling is good or bad or whether it makes sense. For each sensation that comes up, simply accept it as it is — letting go of the need to change it or to understand what it means.

A flowing stream can teach us much about how feelings naturally move. At times a stream runs shallow. At other times, it runs deep. Sometimes it is gentle and slow. Sometimes it reaches the intensity of white-water rapids. Yet a stream keeps moving, even over rocks. If it ever gets dammed up, it becomes stagnant.

In Sense-Feel-Heal, you learn to let the energy of feelings flow like water. It is healing to let them flow rather than to try to control or stop them. As your sensations move and flow, one feeling may lead to another, still-deeper feeling. This may lead to yet another, perhaps lighter feeling. When you open your heart and embrace all your sensations and feelings, you will feel more whole and therefore more safe. In this way, you move to a new level of what it means to feel safe. As your capacity grows for dealing with life as it is, you can let go of outdated notions of control and relax into the sense of personal power that comes from being present in each moment.

Loving Ourselves Where It Hurts

Obviously, we would prefer not to experience upset feelings — or their corresponding body sensations. But if we view unpleasant sensations as a nuisance or a sign of weakness, this attitude will block our emotions from flowing easily, and they will get stuck in our bodies and psyches.

Most people need help learning to take an attitude of empathy and compassion for uncomfortable feelings. But we can learn to embrace them the same way we would embrace our own three-year-old child, whom we love very much, if he or she came into our room feeling upset. If this happened, what would you do? Would you tell your child to stop crying and grow up? Would you tell the child to leave you alone? Or would you simply embrace and hold this precious child? Most of us know in our hearts that ideally we would support this sweet child with our deepest empathy and love.

This is how Sense-Feel-Heal asks you to greet any sensations that show up in your body. Don't reject these feelings or think you shouldn't be feeling them. Embrace each experience as if it were a much-loved child, or perhaps your inner child. This way, you will heal your fear of vulnerability and any tendency you may have toward self-criticism about being too emotional or weak. As a result, you will become more open and less reactive in all your relationships. You will learn to accept the ups and downs of life more gracefully — to accept that pain and upset are natural responses to having our needs frustrated. There is nothing wrong with feeling frustrated. You need comfort, not criticism, when you feel such things.

During a Sense-Feel-Heal session a person may recall forgotten or repressed painful events or upsetting visual or kinesthetic memories. Others simply observe how their sensations change when they give this type of loving attention to whatever they feel. Greet anything you experience with openness and curiosity. If you feel pain, be tender toward yourself and stay with your sensations. Let go of thoughts about why or about what's wrong. And remember to breathe. Do not try to control how your energy moves. People often stop breathing when they feel discomfort, in an unconscious attempt to control or minimize unpleasant sensations. Stay open and pay attention to each sensation as it comes up. If you take this attitude of open, loving attention toward yourself, the energy of your nervous system will learn to travel along its natural path to healing.

When your guide repeats a question about your sensations, even if nothing seems to have changed, report your experience as if it were fresh and new. Avoid repeating something like "It's still the same." Each time your guide asks a question, take a fresh look at what you notice happening in your body.

If a past memory does appear in your awareness, this can be an additional gift to your healing. Working with a past memory offers a way to go even deeper with the practice of loving yourself where it hurts. It also helps you have more empathy and acceptance regarding your core fears so you can reveal these with more depth and clarity during your repair. In the next chapter you will learn more about how to be with any painful memories that come up.

Eric Guides Donna Using Sense-Feel-Heal

In chapter 13, we described how Donna guided Eric in the Sense-Feel-Heal process when he felt performance anxiety in bed. That is an example of how to use this tool in the moment when difficult feelings arise. Doing so allowed Eric to move through his fears — with awareness and compassion — rather than getting flooded and going into a reactive pattern.

The following example shows Eric guiding Donna to repair a reactive incident that got triggered over a long-standing money issue between them. Eric was a tech geek and loved to keep up with the latest in digital technology. Donna thought he spent too much on his electronic toys, far too many of which ended up in the closet after a short time. Eric felt he had the right to get what he wanted, since he was the breadwinner. After many arguments over this issue, they eventually came to an agreement that Eric would check with Donna on any purchases over five hundred dollars.

One day Eric got carried away bidding online on a new tablet computer. He'd wanted it badly for months, but the retail cost was more than double their agreed-upon spending limit, and he felt sheepish sharing his desire with Donna. One day, on his favorite auction site, he saw an opportunity to get it for half price. But during last-minute bidding, Eric impulsively placed a bid far in excess of their agreed spending limit. Not expecting to win, Eric was shocked when he did. Not only had he significantly violated their agreement, Eric then made matters worse by trying to hide all this from Donna.

Of course, she found out. Her immediate impulse was to blow up at Eric for breaking their agreement and trying to hide it from her. Yet, attempting to keep to their most *important* agreement — to deal with reactive incidents using the tools they had — Donna decided to calm herself and approach this matter by asking for a clearing session.

As they reviewed the incident, Donna's upset was apparent: "I'm really angry at you for buying that tablet and not telling me. But under that, I feel deeply hurt. A story comes up in my mind that what matters to me is not important to you, that my feelings don't count, and that I can't count on you because all you ever think about is what you want. I feel so alone right now. I can feel a knot in my stomach. I need to know I matter to you, Eric."

Hearing this, Eric's feelings softened. He said, "I am so sorry you feel this pain. You are so important to me. You are more important than anything. I can't believe I blew it like that. I was just like a kid who had to have his new toy and couldn't think of anything else. I feel awful that I violated our agreement. I am so sorry I didn't come to you and admit I had done that. I am so, so sorry I have hurt you."

Tearing up slightly, Donna responded, "Oh Eric, I know you just got carried away. And I know you have a good heart. But this knot in my stomach comes back when I think my needs aren't important to you, and it ends up hurting so much. I remember feeling this way when my father would break an agreement with me. So many times he promised we would go somewhere and do something, but then when the time came and I was waiting, it was as if he never said it. All he would do is give me excuses. That type of thing still hurts so much."

Eric offered, "Would you like to do the Sense-Feel-Heal process with this? I'd like to do anything I can to help you feel better."

Donna thought this would be helpful, so she moved to a comfortable chair to begin the process. Eric sat across from her with the list of guide questions. Once Donna had relaxed into her chair, Eric prompted her to recall the triggering incident, to restimulate Donna's feelings: "So, recall and describe how you felt when you learned I had bought the tablet computer." Donna replied: "Well, I felt like someone had just punched me in the gut, and I thought you didn't care about me, that I'm just not that important to you."

Eric could tell Donna was getting triggered all over again. Yet his role as guide wasn't to further discuss the issue, or to explain himself, but to help her get in touch with the body sensations associated with the triggering. So, staying in his role as guide, Eric asked, "What body sensations are you aware of as you say these words?

"I feel that knot in my stomach."

"How big is it? Is it more like a grape, an orange, or a melon?"

"About the size of an orange."

"What is its shape?"

"It's sort of like a smashed orange, like someone stepped on the orange."

"As you imagine this smashed orange, what do you notice now?"

"The knot gets bigger, more intense."

"Okay. Can you be with this sensation a bit longer?"

"As I just sit here feeling it, I feel the intensity lessen."

"As you feel this, are there any other changes you notice?"

"The knot is still there. Still shaped sort of like a smashed orange."

"And is it heavy or light?"

"It's kind of heavy."

"Cool or warm?"

"Hmmm...I can't tell."

"That's okay. Is there any pressure with it?"

"Yes. It's kind of pushing backward toward my back."

"So it is heavy and pushing backward."

"Yes."

"You're doing great, honey. Are you willing to stay with this for a bit longer? Can we just be curious what will happen next?"

"Okay."

After a minute, Eric asked, "Can you describe what's happening now? What sensations do you notice in your body?"

"The knot has gotten larger and tighter. I see some images of me when my father forgot my ninth birthday."

"Can you stay with these images, and notice what you experience in your body?"

"Now the knot has gotten larger and is starting to churn. In my mind's eye, I see myself at nine years old, sitting alone in our dining room feeling kinda panicky."

"Can you allow these feelings and sensations to just be there? Can you just be present to what you're feeling?"

"Yes."

"Would you like some supportive touch?"

"Yes, I'd like that."

"Show me exactly where the knot is. I'd like to sit next to you and put my hand on top of the knot. Do you want me to do that, honey?"

"Yes, I'd like that." Donna took his hand and put it on her belly. Eric relaxed next to her and sensed Donna's stomach area with his palm. He offered her a steady, firm touch. During their first Sense-Feel-Heal sessions, Eric would rub or massage Donna, as if he could fix what was going on inside her. But they learned that this type of motion only stimulates further agitation in an upset nervous system. Now Eric remembered to concentrate on relaxing his own nervous system and holding a steady touch.

This is how coregulation works. Donna's nervous system slowly downloaded Eric's relaxed state into her body — automatically and in its own time — and this resulted in changes in her body sensations. This is identical to how a parent's supportive touch calms and soothes an upset child. It's a biological process that exists in all of us, regardless of age. With Eric's nurturing support, Donna could more easily embrace this younger part of her nervous system and heal the inner historical wound that had gotten triggered.

Eventually, Eric sensed a tightening in Donna's muscles. Soon after, he also felt a buzzing energy, a kind of electrical tingling, in his palm. He sat quietly, sensing his palm connecting with Donna's nervous system. As he relaxed more, he noticed Donna becoming calm and relaxed. A moment later Donna breathed more deeply into her belly and let out a sigh, as if releasing some of the tightness.

Eric asked, "What are you noticing now, Donna?"

"I feel sadness. Some tears are coming."

Eric knew it was important for him to accept and supportively be with anything that arose in Donna. Rather than try to console her, Eric said, "Can you stay with your tears, your sadness?"

Donna allowed tears to stream down her face, shaking slightly.

"I'm here for you, honey," Eric said.

In a few minutes, Donna's tears subsided, and she took a deep breath.

"What are you experiencing now?" Eric asked.

"The knot has loosened up and shrunk down to the size of an egg."

"You're doing great. Can we just stay with it a bit longer and see what happens next?"

"Okay. Thank you so much for being here with me."

"There's nowhere else I'd rather be. You're the most important person in my life, Donna."

After a minute more, Donna's belly had entirely relaxed. She opened her eyes and looked at Eric, who was gazing back with smiling eyes.

Donna said, "You are so wonderful. I'm so grateful that you are my guy. Thank you for holding me and helping me feel safe enough to go into this. I love you so much."

In this way, Eric and Donna turned a reactive incident into a process to heal past childhood wounds. In addition, they found that the more they integrated Sense-Feel-Heal into their clearing sessions and repair process, they experienced fewer reactive incidents, and the ones that happened were less intense and more easily repaired.

Using Sense-Feel-Heal as Partners in Cohealing

Serving as guide for each other can be very healing. Couples come to experience their relationship as a safe harbor where they have permission to feel all their feelings — something they may never have experienced before.

Sense-Feel-Heal embraces and heals wounds that reside deep in the unconscious mind. If partners can be present and guide each other in this way, they will find a level of transformation and soulful connection that they never imagined possible.

Some couples even use this practice as a weekly bonding and healing ritual. When you take turns being each other's guide in this process, it builds each of your capacities to be present to the state of both of your nervous systems.

Not all couples will choose to do Sense-Feel-Heal with each other. If your partner is not available for this, or if you are single, you can do it with a friend. Or you can do it alone, asking the guide's questions silently to yourself (for more on this, see chapter 15).

Note that the first time you try Sense-Feel-Heal, it might not go as smoothly as the example with Donna and Eric. You might feel awkward as the guide. Or you might not achieve a clear resolution. This is normal. Like most things, this technique takes practice. Be patient with yourself and trust that anything you do is going to be helpful. Regard the instructions in this chapter as a map of possible places to visit. Take your time, be curious, and feel free to improvise and experiment.

As you continue to practice the Sense-Feel-Heal process, your inner sensing will become more refined. You will feel safer going into unknown territory. You will get better at noticing what is going on inside of you. As you start, know that the only thing you need for healing is a genuine curiosity and a willingness to feel whatever comes up.

Sometimes, the shift that marks the completion of this process can be subtle, such as a sigh or a simple relaxation in your breathing. At other times, the shifts may be more dramatic. You may feel energy moving through your body in an almost electrical way. Your body may even begin to move or shake. These are typically good signs of releasing energy that has been locked in your body for years. You may see visual images that correspond to this energy, such as brighter colors or dancing light. Later, you may notice that you feel and act differently in a situation that would normally trigger reactivity or fear. You may feel safer, more trusting, and more self-accepting.

Do not expect that all Sense-Feel-Heal sessions will go the same way. While similar themes may recur, each session is entirely unique. Let go of preconceptions and expectations. Just be open and see what shows up.

Chapter Fifteen

Compassionate Self-Inquiry
for Inner Healing

MOST OF THE HEALING AND REPAIR practices in this book are designed for partners to use together. This chapter offers a practice that you can use on your own to heal your core fears. The process is similar to a self-guided Sense-Feel-Heal session, but it guides you even further into clearing emotional wounds that trigger reactive incidents. It is called *Compassionate Self-Inquiry*.

A good time to use this practice is during a pause, when you are taking time away from your partner in preparation for your repair session. You can also use it whenever you are upset and you cannot repair together with your partner. Or you can use it on your own to heal past upsetting events — from a former relationship or from childhood. Anyone, whether single or in a relationship, can use this practice regularly to become more open and less fearful about the risks involved in a loving relationship.

Compassionate Self-Inquiry

Before beginning the process described below, find a location where you feel safe and physically comfortable and where you won't be interrupted. Ideally, the space should allow you to lie down if you want. Bring things you find especially soothing (like a soft blanket, a big pillow, or a favorite object like a stuffed doll or animal). Once you've arranged your location, take a moment and use your favorite self-calming tool from chapter 3 — feel yourself supported by your chair, track your breathing, relax deeply.

To start the Compassionate Self-Inquiry process, identify a specific triggering incident to explore. As practice for your first session, choose only a mildly upsetting incident from an adult relationship in your past. Once you are familiar and comfortable with the practice, use it with any recent triggering incident or past issue.

Recall the Triggering Incident

Recall the setting and circumstances of the triggering incident. What did the other person do or say that triggered you? Remember the scene in as much vivid detail as you can. Try to hear the words and see the actions. What did you want from this person? What did you sense and feel? As you recall the upset feeling, notice your body sensations in the moment. What is happening right now in your chest, belly, throat, and heart? Put the palm of your hand on top of those sensations as an act of self-nurturing. Or use both arms and give yourself a hug, embracing your sensations or feelings as a nurturing parent would embrace a hurting child.

Or, imagine that this upset part of you is a more tender, vulnerable aspect of yourself. With compassion, witness this upset or hurting part of yourself while you hold it with a spacious, nurturing attitude. Stay with whatever you are feeling for as long as you need, giving yourself empathy for any pain, fear, frustration, or disappointment. As you do this, remember to breathe fully and deeply. You are making space for your upset self to more fully experience things you may not have felt at the time. Track your body sensations using the guidance in the Sense-Feel-Heal practice (see chapter 14).

Be Aware of Any Feelings, Stories, or Memories That Arise

As you continue tracking what you are feeling, notice how your body sensations change or move. Also, be aware of any stories or beliefs that come up in your mind. Embrace these with compassion. Slowly go through the memory, as if reviewing a video that you can pause.

You may want to wrap yourself in a blanket, or to lie down with a blanket and pillow, as a way to comfort yourself. As you explore your recently activated feelings, you may sense that you are also comforting a younger self within you who probably experienced similar feelings in childhood. Sometimes when you do this self-inquiry on a current incident, you may get clear images of a scene from childhood. If this happens, it is a gift for deeper inner healing. It offers you an opportunity to work with the root of your trigger. You may choose to shift your focus to this childhood memory and use the practice to nurture and heal that younger part of yourself, giving your younger self permission to more fully feel what it felt then. This time, however, no one is going to tell you to stop crying or stop being upset. Instead, make room for your younger self to get closure or completion on something that has been buried or suppressed.

Whether or not an earlier memory surfaces, allow yourself to feel and express whatever comes up. Imagine speaking to the other person involved in the situation, saying whatever you wish you could have said then. Speak out loud if you wish. Let yourself shout or cry if you are moved to.

You may also feel moved to speak soothing words to your tender, vulnerable self or to your younger self. Let these words be nurturing and empathetic, like: "Wow, that was intense. You showed a lot of courage to let yourself go there." Or, "I love you. I'm here for you." If words do not come to you, that's okay, too.

Identify Any Needs Beneath the Emotions

Give yourself time to experience whatever feelings flow through you. Feel the frustration, hurt, anger, disappointment, helplessness, fear, or shock. As you do, consider what core needs or fears might be triggering these feelings. If you are feeling anger, what need is, or was, frustrated? Feel this need and your longing to have this need met. Feel the pain about not having what you want or need.

Remember that it is a healing act to give yourself loving attention when you feel hurt or upset. Rocking, hugging, patting, touching, and stroking are all ways to show caring and nurturing toward yourself. Take your time.

Stay Calm and Centered

If the feelings get too intense, back off a bit and refocus on your calming practices. Reassure yourself that you are safe. Feel the chair or the floor supporting you. Open your eyes and look around the room. Focus on something in the room and take a moment to examine it in detail. Do conscious breathing. Feel your arms around yourself. Allow the sensations in your heart area to expand and be felt — as if opening your heart to this much-loved aspect of your conditioned self. When you feel calm enough, return to tracking the body sensations and feelings associated with this memory.

Return Slowly to the Present Moment

Be with yourself like this for as long as it feels supportive and nurturing. After you have reexperienced this memory and have nurtured yourself through these feelings, then you are ready to bring it to a close. Find a comfortable, restful position for your body, and take about ten slow, deep breaths. Then, get up slowly — but only when you feel like it. Be gentle with yourself; don't hurry. Look around and reorient to your surroundings. Walk around a bit, sensing your body. Give yourself appreciation for letting yourself have this experience.

Digesting Small Pieces of the Original Experience

As the nervous system discharges the stuck energy patterns of an upsetting memory, it can be natural to feel shaking, temperature shifts, or pulsing energy waves. These things indicate that your emotional energy is flowing again, so if you experience any of them, don't worry. Just go with it and know that it is part of the healing process and it will gradually subside. If you need to calm yourself at any time during the process, practice a relaxation technique.

A current approach in trauma recovery methodology is that healing from early wounding occurs little by little. It is not necessary or even advisable to go all the way into the remembered painful experience in one session. That can retraumatize your nervous system. The best way to achieve a complete healing is to do this practice little by little, a bit at a time, and anytime or whenever one of your buttons gets pushed.

Self-Inquiry Before a Five-Minute Relationship Repair

As mentioned above, it can be very helpful for both partners to do a Compassionate Self-Inquiry during the pause phase that might precede the Five-Minute Relationship Repair process (see chapter 10). In this way, you would use your pause to connect with your upset feelings and notice if any earlier memories arise that relate to your current upset.

Afterward, you would both then fill out your Repair Statements and share them with each other. Your repair process will go much more smoothly if you have done this self-inquiry practice first — because it helps you take full responsibility for your own sensitivities and buttons. It also builds confidence that you can handle the normal frustrations that come with a relationship. This helps you avoid the trap of thinking you or your partner has done something bad or wrong if one of you is upset. Upsets happen. No one is to blame. No one is bad or wrong.

When partners share their discoveries about the origins of their triggers and buttons, this helps them have more empathy for each other. As partners know each other more deeply and realize the impact of their childhood wounds, they can overcome the tendency to take each other's reactive behavior personally.

This information about each other also helps you know what to say and do to reassure your partner when old fears get triggered. Simple key statements like "I think you're good enough exactly the way you are" or "Your feelings are important to me" can help make up for what each of you did not receive as children. Such reassurances help heal any insecure attachment circuits and build a secure emotional bond.

Letting yourself feel emotional pain is healing because you give yourself permission to experience and move some emotional energy that you may never have allowed yourself to feel before. Most of us, as children, came to believe that if we were in pain, something was bad or wrong about us. This is because our caregivers often tried to distract us from our pain or get us to override our upset feelings. So we learned early on to either shut down or amp up our feelings, which offered little chance for our upsets to receive the nurturing reassurances we needed. When we lovingly embrace our upsets, we offer ourselves the corrective emotional experience that allows our feelings to resolve naturally.

Some Cautions and Reminders

In practicing Compassionate Self-Inquiry, you might notice a tendency to shut down as you begin to experience deeply buried feelings. For instance, you may find yourself trying to understand why something happened rather than simply feeling what you felt. This sort of resistance to uncomfortable feelings is normal. Just go as far as you can with this practice. Encourage the hurting part of yourself to feel and express your hurt, knowing that your adult awareness is witnessing this with acceptance and compassion. It takes many repetitions to rewire your nervous system, so be patient.

Sometimes people say, "But what if I have a tendency to become impatient with myself? What if I don't like the wounded part of me? What if I view this part of me as a nuisance or think I shouldn't be so sensitive or insecure?"

If this happens with you, notice what you feel as you observe your inner critic. Imagine the interaction as if you were watching a parent and child. What would you feel if a mother told her crying child to grow up or get over it? Does it change what you feel if you see yourself from this perspective? If you feel sadness, this is a good start. That's the beginning of a softer, more empathetic attitude toward yourself.

If you do this practice regularly, you will heal your triggers over time. For now, just accept that your core feelings and needs will be suppressed at the time of a reactive incident, and you will have a tendency to react. Learn to pause as soon as you notice reactivity. And use Compassionate Self-Inquiry to help get back to being your more resourceful self.

By now, you know that relationships provide fertile ground for having your buttons pushed. Each time you get triggered, see if you can welcome it as part of your healing process — as a window into what still needs healing.

Nature gives us what we need to heal ourselves. The problem is we think we know better, so we try to control what's natural and substitute what's comfortable to our egos. The self-healing tools in this book give us practice using what nature has given us — our feelings and our ability to express and move stuck energy.

Get used to revealing to your partner when you get triggered, either in the moment or even days or weeks afterward. This helps you relax into the fact that you do have buttons, and so does your partner, and that having your buttons get pushed is forgivable, human, and normal.

When you can openly admit you have buttons, you won't feel the need to hide your weaknesses. You'll be less defensive. You won't be afraid of being found out, of looking bad, or of not being perfect. Having nothing to hide is a great boon to self-trust and to feeling safe in your relationship and in your life. To paraphrase a famous song, you may even come to recognize that "freedom's just another word for nothing left to hide."

Chapter Sixteen

Make a Plan for a Secure Partnership

IF YOU WANT TO BUILD A SECURE, lasting partnership, you need to be able to work out differences, misunderstandings, and reactive incidents. To achieve this, start by making a conscious plan for integrating the tools in this book into your daily life. You have learned about pausing, calming your nervous system, coregulating, reassuring safety, and repairing upsets. This chapter reviews the basic principles and practices you need to create a life of lasting love.

If you are reading this book with your partner, look through the checklist below together and talk about how you can implement each of these practices. If you are reading on your own, visualize how you might practice these in a current or future relationship.

Also, as you start to use these tools in your life, remember that upsets and triggering situations vary, and each person responds differently. Sometimes you will be able to repair distress quickly, on the spot. At other times, you or your partner may get triggered more intensely, and it may take a longer time to recover and then repair. You may even need to spend time apart before fully repairing a reactive incident. Ultimately, the goal is simply to catch a reactive cycle as quickly as possible — so that distress doesn't build up — calm your survival alarms, and repair ruptures as soon as you can.

Finally, be kind and gentle to yourselves and each other. You are learning new tools, and there is going to be a learning curve. It's all about repetition and consistency. The more you practice these tools, the more effective you will become. Consistently using these tools over time will rewire each of your brains to increase loving behaviors with each other and diminish reactive cycles.

Checklist of Tips and Practices

Coregulate Frequently: Share supportive touch, eye contact, soothing voice tones, and reassuring messages — frequently. Make sure to physically connect every day, especially at times of greeting and departure. Learn your partner's core needs and core fears, and whenever you detect distress, move to coregulate each other accordingly (see chapter 4).

Recognize Your Reactive Cycle: Be alert for characteristic signs of reactivity: body sensations, stories, reactive feelings, and reactive behaviors. Don't believe stories, whether yours or your partner's. Learn to recognize when either of you is triggered or experiencing distress (see chapter 8). When you do, use Pause-Calm-Repair (see below).

Use Your Pause Signal: Whenever you sense distress or triggering in either partner, call for a pause. Establish an agreed-upon pause signal and use it (see chapter 2). Once either person becomes reactive, don't keep talking or you will land in the Hole. Know that when survival alarms are ringing, you will probably unintentionally trigger each other more.

Calm and Nurture Yourself: During a pause, calm yourself. Practice and master at least one self-calming tool (see chapter 3). By feeling a chair hold you or tracking your breathing, you will rewire your nervous system to have better brakes. Give yourself loving attention when your core fears or insecurities are triggered (see also chapters 14 and 15).

Commit to Repair: Agree that you will use the Five-Minute Relationship Repair process (see chapter 10) after any reactive episode. Do this as soon as you can. Until you are well-practiced with the process, follow the Repair Statement script, using the words and phrases we've provided for reactive behaviors, core fears and needs, and so on (see the appendices).

Use the Talker-Listener Structure: When you repair, take turns being talker and listener. Be disciplined in these roles, and do not interrupt. When you are the talker, use the Repair Statement script (see chapter 10). If you are the listener, engage in responsive listening and use the guidelines for a reassuring response (see appendix A). To facilitate learning to communicate and repair, stay with these scripts. Don't improvise.

Speak from Your Vulnerable Core: Make it a practice to report your core feelings and core needs to your partner. Remember that underneath your anger, your defensiveness, your stories, and your interpretations lie softer, more vulnerable feelings like hurt, sadness, and fear. Practice speaking this way by using the Repair Statement script.

Calm and Reassure Your Partner: Know the key statements that work best to reassure your partner. Review the guidelines for a reassuring response (see chapter 10). Learn the type of supportive touch and eye contact that calms your partner. Quickly offer reassurances whenever you sense your partner is triggered. When a pause is called during a triggering incident, do something to calm each other, like hugging or saying, "We are okay here. We will repair this." That will help each of you calm yourselves faster and enable a quicker repair.

Seek Mutually Beneficial Solutions: Remember, a relationship is like a three-legged race: it is in each person's best interest to solve all issues in ways that work for both partners. Manipulating your partner to do things *your* way will backfire on you. After you resolve a difference or issue, check in with each other to make sure you both feel good about the resolution or decision.

Clear the Air Regularly: Use the clearing practice in chapter 11 on a regularly scheduled basis to make sure you do not let resentments, unresolved reactive incidents, or unspoken needs build up into a barrage of upset and reactivity.

Use the Sense-Feel-Heal Process: Guide each other to transform upset feelings by giving loving attention to body sensations and core feelings — moving out of the storytelling mind and into direct awareness of your nervous system. Use the Sense-Feel-Heal process to heal each other's old emotional wounds, sensitivities, and buttons (see chapter 14).

Use Compassionate Self-Inquiry: Work with your reactions as important opportunities for self-healing using Compassionate Self-Inquiry (see chapter 15). Give yourself loving attention and supportive touch whenever you feel triggered. Gently revisit what was too painful or scary to feel as a child.

Get Online Support from the Authors of This Book: To get additional clearing and communication tools, including video demonstrations with real couples, visit the authors' website, www.fiveminuterelationshiprepair.com. In addition to the online workbook that accompanies this book, this website offers free quizzes, checklists, worksheets, and webinars to support your continuing learning and growth.

Create a Vision Statement for Your Relationship

Once you understand the tools and practices in this book, sit down with your partner and make a plan for how you will apply these tools in your relationship. Create a vision statement for how you will deal with distress from now on. If you're reading this on your own, envision what you want in a current or future relationship.

Basically, this is an agreement about how you intend to operate as a couple. Even though you will probably slip up at times and unconsciously fall into your reactive cycle, it is important to have a clear plan to guide you and help you get back on track. There is no standard format for a vision statement. It can be written in whatever way you like. However, it should be as specific as possible, naming the specific tools and actions you will both take to cope with and repair conflict and reactive behavior. Both of you should sign this statement.

As an example, below is the vision statement that Eric and Donna created. As they successfully used the techniques in this book to catch and stop their reactive cycles, they agreed that they needed to put down their sword and shield and communicate core feelings and needs. Donna and Eric dedicated themselves to using the Repair Statement and other clearing tools on a regular basis, and they decided to put their shared vision in writing. This served as a new road map for how they would deal with differences, upsets, and reactive incidents. Read over their vision statement below and talk with your partner about the principles you'd like to include in your own plan.

Donna and Eric's Vision Statement

We dedicate ourselves to building a secure bond where we can grow emotionally, heal our triggers, be happy together, and experience our relationship as a safe haven.

We each came into the relationship with unhealed wounds and insecurities from the past. These old buttons and sensitivities will get triggered, but this does not mean we are unlovable or incapable of loving. Nor does it mean we don't love each other. When our old fears get triggered, we will look for what they can teach us about ourselves and each other. We will view these difficulties as opportunities for healing and growth.

We agree to operate in line with these, our "Ten Commandments":

1. If either of us is triggered, we will ask to pause. Then we will calm ourselves and, if possible, offer coregulation and reassurance to calm each other.

2. We will catch our reactive communication and stop it before it escalates. We will look for the softer feelings and needs underneath more aggressive or defensive feelings.

3. We will use the Repair Statement script whenever there is a reactive incident so we can repair it and get back to feeling safe together.

4. We will keep learning to better express our core feelings, fears, and needs — even when we are not engaged in repair. We will build emotional intimacy and trust by being transparent about the things that trouble us — before these things build up.

5. We will appreciate and reassure each other when we disclose our vulnerable, softer parts, by giving the reassuring response the other needs to feel safe and secure.

6. We will use the talker-listener structure whenever we discuss difficult issues, slowing down our communication so we really hear each other.

7. We will make it our regular practice to check in with each other and clear the air once a week. We will also do this spontaneously as the need arises.

8. We will connect every day with some type of physical and emotional coregulation, including hugs and acknowledgments.

9. We will make fairness, mutuality, and equality our primary values. We will decide all matters and resolve all issues in a way that works for both of us.

10. We are going to make mistakes, trip up, and accidentally trigger each other. Whenever that happens, we will forgive ourselves and quickly remind each other to return to the practices on this list.

Signed, Donna and Eric

Knowing that you are committed to a shared vision will support you to show up in a new way when someone gets triggered. Signing this agreement symbolizes that you have permission to remind each other to get back on track whenever anyone slips up or forgets. This vision will remind you of the mutually beneficial purpose of working with reactive incidents in a new, conscious, and compassionate way. Following this plan turns your partnership into the safe harbor your loving hearts so deeply desire.

Appendix A

The Five-Minute Repair Process

The Repair Statement

Note: To fill in the blanks in the Repair Statement, see the appropriate categories in the appendix B reference lists.

"I'd like to repair something with you. Is this a good time?

"I got triggered when I heard you say (or saw you do)

_____

[name your partner's specific words or actions].

"A story came up in my mind that _____
[describe your *reactive story*].

"I reacted by _____
[describe your *reactive behavior*].

"But deep down inside, I felt _____
[name your *core feeling*].

"A fear came up in me that _____
[name your *core fear*].

"What I needed more than anything was to feel _____
_____ [name your *core need*].

"I am sorry I reacted that way and would like to take it back.

"If I could do it over again, I would have told you that I was feeling _____
[repeat your *core feeling* and *core fear*].

"And I would have asked for reassurance that _____
[repeat your *core need*]."

The Reassuring Response

As a listener, when offering a reassuring response, first repeat back what you heard your partner say. Include the core feeling, core fear, and core need your partner revealed in the last part of his or her statement. With an attitude of understanding and empathy, say to your partner something like the following:

"What I heard you say was that you felt _____
[repeat your partner's *core feeling* and *core fear*].

"And you needed reassurance that _____
[repeat your partner's *core need*]."

Use the actual words your partner said, leaving out your own interpretations, stories, corrections, judgments, disputes, and self-defense.

Follow your recap with these questions:

"Did I get everything you said?"
"Is there anything you want to correct or add?"

If your partner reports that you missed something, simply try again until he or she is satisfied.

Next, if appropriate, deliver a simple apology. Using supportive touch, look into your partner's eyes, and speak in a soothing, slow voice. Say something like:

"I'm so sorry I hurt you."

Finally, deliver a message that reassures any core fears or core needs your partner revealed in the Repair Statement. When you speak, look into your partner's left eye and slowly repeat your statement three times, with pauses in between. Use simple statements like the examples below:

"You're the most important person in my life."
"You are more important to me than anything."
"I need you very much."
"I can't imagine life without you."
"I'll never leave you."
"You can't get rid of me."
"I'm in this for the long haul."
"I care deeply how you feel."
"Your happiness is very important to me."
"You are great just the way you are."
"I feel lucky to have found you."
"You're the most wonderful partner in the world."
"You're the best thing that ever happened to me."
"You are more than good enough."
"You are irreplaceable."
"You are my hero."
"I love you just the way you are."
"I appreciate you for all you do for me and us."

Appendix B

Reference Lists of Reactive Cycle Elements

Reactive Behaviors

- ❖ Try to fix the problem with logic, solve it rationally
- ❖ Agree insincerely, placate
- ❖ Rationalize, intellectualize to avoid emotions
- ❖ Make a joke or cute remark, laugh it off
- ❖ Ignore, pretend it doesn't matter or you didn't hear
- ❖ Avoid, distance yourself
- ❖ Leave, walk out, move away
- ❖ Withdraw, hide out
- ❖ Act confused, freeze up, space out, shut down
- ❖ Correct other person, argue the point, debate
- ❖ Defend yourself
- ❖ Ridicule, get sarcastic
- ❖ Make insulting noises or faces, roll your eyes
- ❖ Talk over the other, interrupt
- ❖ Repeat yourself
- ❖ Get sullen or sulk

- ❖ Mutter to yourself
- ❖ Compare partner to someone "better"
- ❖ Label, judge, name-call
- ❖ Complain
- ❖ Criticize
- ❖ Lecture, teach, preach
- ❖ Pursue, push, pressure, prod, provoke
- ❖ Talk loudly in an anxious tone
- ❖ Interrogate, question, ask for explanations
- ❖ Try to prove you are right
- ❖ Attack or blame
- ❖ Yell, blow up
- ❖ Guilt trip

Reactive Stories

In these phrases, change the pronouns "he" and "she" to suit your situation.

"I am all alone."
"He shuts me out."
"She is so distant."
"I am way down on the list."
"I always come last."
"He just doesn't seem to care."
"My feelings don't matter."
"We are never close anymore."
"She is not that into me."
"I am just not sure I matter."
"It's like he doesn't see me."
"I don't know how to reach her."
"If I didn't push, we'd never be close."
"He doesn't really need me at all."

"Nothing I do is ever enough."

"She doesn't appreciate me."

"I can never get it right, so I give up."

"I must be flawed somehow."

"I feel like a failure as a mate."

"It just all seems so hopeless."

"I try to keep everything calm."

"I try not to rock the boat."

"I go into my shell where it's safe."

"I am just not as needy."

"She just gets overemotional."

"I can handle things on my own."

"I don't know what he is talking about. We're fine."

"I try to fix things, to solve the problem."

Reactive Feelings

Fight
- ❖ annoyed
- ❖ irritated
- ❖ frustrated
- ❖ angry
- ❖ resentful
- ❖ infuriated

Flight
- ❖ nervous
- ❖ worried
- ❖ insecure
- ❖ anxious
- ❖ fearful
- ❖ panicked

Freeze

* hopeless
* confused
* ashamed
* stuck
* numb
* paralyzed

Body Sensations

Some examples are:

* a knot in your stomach
* feeling heat or coldness
* a tightness somewhere
* a constriction or pounding in your chest or belly
* a lump in your throat
* a weight on your shoulders
* a heavy feeling
* a fluttering sensation
* a pain in your heart
* shakiness
* tension

Core Feelings

* sad
* hurt
* pained
* grief-stricken
* lonely

Core Fears

I'm afraid of being...
- ❖ abandoned
- ❖ rejected
- ❖ left
- ❖ all alone
- ❖ unneeded
- ❖ insignificant
- ❖ invisible
- ❖ ignored
- ❖ unimportant
- ❖ flawed
- ❖ blamed
- ❖ not good enough
- ❖ inadequate
- ❖ a failure
- ❖ unlovable
- ❖ controlled
- ❖ trapped
- ❖ overwhelmed
- ❖ suffocated
- ❖ out of control
- ❖ helpless
- ❖ weak

Core Needs

I need to feel...
- ❖ connected to you
- ❖ accepted by you

- ❖ valued by you
- ❖ appreciated by you
- ❖ respected by you
- ❖ needed by you
- ❖ that you care about me
- ❖ that I matter to you
- ❖ that we are a team
- ❖ that I can count on you
- ❖ that I can reach out for you
- ❖ that you'll comfort me if I'm in distress
- ❖ that you'll be there if I need you

Acknowledgments

FIRST, WE THANK ALL THE COUPLES we have had the honor to work with over the past four decades: In your courage to open and grow, each of you has offered us the opportunity to discover what partners need to make love thrive.

Next, we want to thank Peter Levine: Your development of Somatic Experiencing as an approach to healing trauma expanded our ability to help partners coheal through coregulation and holding presence for each other's inner experiences.

We also want to thank Sue Johnson: Your development of Emotionally Focused Therapy for couples increased our understanding of how reactive cycles operate and how to help partners express their core feelings, fears, and needs.

A special thanks goes to Stan Tatkin for his development of the Psychobiological Approach to Couples Therapy: The priority you place on partners being good guardians of their couple bubble solidified our emphasis on coregulation and the need for quick repair. You inspired us to see how partners can rewire each other's brains so that they can function securely as a couple in love.

We want to also thank many other contributors to our thinking: Carl Rogers, Carl Jung, Fritz Perls, John Grinder, Milton Erickson, Helen Palmer, John Bowlby, Stephen Porges, Roberto Assagioli.

Finally, we want to thank the tireless researchers in the fields of neuroscience and attachment theory: Your studies have helped us embrace the emerging attachment-based paradigm for helping couples reduce distress, operate more securely, and maximize their mutual happiness.

Index

About the Authors

SUSAN CAMPBELL received her PhD in clinical psychology from the University of Massachusetts, where she became a member of that school's prestigious graduate faculty and founded that school's couple and family therapy graduate program. She has also received extensive postdoctoral training in couple and family therapy, group dynamics, organization development, Gestalt therapy, Neuro-Linguistic Programming (NLP), psychosynthesis, Buddhist and nondual psychologies, and Jungian therapy.

A faculty member at the Gestalt Institute of San Francisco, Susan trains coaches and therapists throughout the United States and Europe to integrate the tools in this book into their professional practices. In her own practice, she works with singles, couples, coworkers, and work teams to help them communicate respectfully and responsibly when conflicts arise or when buttons get pushed. Her groundbreaking book, *The Couples Journey: Intimacy as a Path to Wholeness,* published in 1980, was the first popular book that introduced mainstream audiences to the idea of relationship as a spiritual practice.

She is the creator and publisher of four entertaining and educational card games for teens, adults, couples, work teams, and singles. Susan's work with couples has been featured on national television, including CNN's *News Night*, *Good Morning America*, and the *Dr. Dean Edell* show, and she has been published widely in popular magazines, such as *Self*, *New Woman*, and *Cosmopolitan*. In 2003–4, she was the couples therapist on the reality TV show *Truth in Love*.

A trained sex therapist, Susan is coauthor of *Revitalizing Sexual Intimacy: How to Keep Your Love Passionate, Alive, and Real*. As an internationally known professional speaker, she speaks to corporate audiences and leads public seminars throughout the United States and in Europe as well as over the Internet. She lives in Sonoma County, California. For more, visit www.susancampbell .com.

JOHN GREY received his PhD in psychology from Stanford University and subsequently cofounded the prestigious Stanford Center for Computer Research in Music and Acoustics (CCRMA). His study of how the brain processes musical sound influenced the development of electronic keyboards and the birth of digital music technologies we take for granted today.

Since 1980, John has been in private practice as a relationship coach specializing in intensive couples retreats as well as a trainer of therapists. He has taught workshops in communication skills and relationship tools at the Esalen Institute, the University of California at Berkeley, Stanford University Business School, and the Scripps Institute.

John has extensive training in a number of modalities. He collaborated with Neuro-Linguistic Programming (NLP) founder John Grinder and presented NLP training programs for therapists and other helping professionals. Over the years, he has integrated into his approach psychosynthesis, Ericksonian hypnotherapy, the Enneagram personality system, Peter Levine's Somatic Experiencing, Buddhist and nondual psychologies, Sue Johnson's Emotionally Focused Therapy (EFT) for couples, and Stan Tatkin's Psychobiological Approach to Couples Therapy (PACT). John is currently a core faculty member of the PACT Institute, a training program for couples therapists.

John has written two previous books on love and relationships: *Becoming Soulmates* and *Relationship Tools for Positive Change*. He created an educational card game for couples, *The Joy of Relationship Cards*. This was turned into an interactive, online self-help system called the *Soulmate Oracle* and was featured on major websites as well as on his own site. His work has also appeared on national television and in popular magazines.

Find out more about John's intensive couples retreats and relationship coaching, as well as his books, blog, and other self-help tools, at his website, www.soulmateoracle.com.

Susan and John are continuing to develop and refine the tools and worksheets in this book. To stay current and get ongoing support, visit www.fiveminuterelationshiprepair.com, where you can get free, printable versions of the exercises, lists, and appendices from this book in the form of a companion workbook. There you will also find additional clearing and communication tools, video demonstrations, quizzes, checklists, worksheets, and information about upcoming webinars to support your growth.